WRATH UNLEASHED™

PRIMA'S OFFICIAL STRATEGY GUIDE

BRYAN STRATTON

PRIMA GAMES
A DIVISION OF RANDOM HOUSE, INC.

3000 LAVA RIDGE COURT
ROSEVILLE, CA 95661
1-800-733-3000
WWW.PRIMAGAMES.COM

CONTENTS

PRIMA'S OFFICIAL STRATEGY GUIDE

INTRODUCTION
WELCOME TO WRATH UNLEASHED™

Thank you for purchasing Prima's Official Strategy Guide to LucasArts' *Wrath Unleashed*. This guide contains all the tips, tricks, strategies, and secrets you need to conquer every World Map and defeat every enemy in the game.

This introductory section gives you a general overview of the controls and in-game help system, and a quick look at the game modes. However, that's just the beginning. Refer to the following sections of the guide for in-depth information.

Note
The PlayStation®2 and Xbox® versions are identical except controls, and everything in this guide applies to either version of the game.

wrath unleashed chapter 1

introduction
- *welcome*
- *basic controls*
- *in game help*
- *game modes*

Overlords and Creatures
Your army can contain any of 32 creatures. This section has the lowdown on all of them, from their hit points to their signature attacks. It also reveals all the attributes and attacks for the four Overlords' Demigod and God modes.

Getting Started
Before you begin playing, take a look at this section, which tells you how to create and manage player profiles, save and load game data, set game options, and fight and win battles. It also contains an overview of Tutorial mode, which we definitely recommend that you check out before playing.

Magic Spells
This section tells you everything you need to know about the eight magic spells you can cast in battles. Using these spells effectively can mean the difference between victory and defeat, so don't overlook this section!

chapter 1
INTRODUCTION

World Maps

Battle Mode and Army Builder
This section covers the one- to four-player Battle game mode, as well as the Army Builder mode, which is used to create custom armies for Battle games.

World Maps
For complete information on all 17 (+ 4 locked) Battle mode World Maps, look no further than this section. It contains basic and advanced strategies for each map, and it also tells you how to unlock the four locked maps: Frenzy, Red 5, Grandmaster, and Checkered.

CAMPAIGN MODE

Campaign Mode
Campaign mode is the meat of the single-player experience. This section describes each of the 16 Campaign mode missions in detail, including all the strategy you need to beat each and unlock the hidden items they hold.

ARENA COMBAT TRAINING

Arena Combat Training
Knowing how to fight arena battles is the key to victory. Consider this section your basic training. It has complete details for all 11 Battle arenas. Not only does it tell you what's most important to do in arena combat, but it also gives you a comprehensive list of what you should *not* do.

chapter 9
VERSUS AND TEAM FIGHTER MODES

Versus and Team Fighter Modes
This section gives you the skinny on Versus mode and Team Fighter mode, the game modes that give you nothing but arena combat.

Game Secrets
The contents of this section are so super-secret that we're not even going to tell you about them in this introduction! You have to turn to the back of the book if you want to find out how to unlock hidden World Maps, Battle arenas, bonus gallery images, medals, and Overlord God modes.

chapter 1

chapter 2

chapter 3

chapter 4

chapter 5

chapter 6

chapter 7

chapter 8

chapter 9

chapter 10

chapter 1

chapter 2

chapter 3

chapter 4

chapter 5

chapter 6

chapter 7

chapter 8

chapter 9

chapter 10

PRIMA'S OFFICIAL STRATEGY GUIDE

BASIC CONTROLS

Xbox®

MENU CONTROLS (XBOX®)

Button	Command
Ⓛ	Highlight menu option
Ⓐ	Confirm selection
Ⓑ	Cancel selection/back up one menu

WORLD MAP CONTROLS (XBOX®)

Button	Command
Ⓛ	Move cursor/highlight selection
Ⓐ	Confirm selection
Ⓑ	Cancel selection/command
Ⓧ	Activate gate (when your selected character is on it)
Ⓨ	In-game help for selected tile
Ⓛ	Zoom out
Ⓡ	Zoom in
Ⓡ or Ⓡ	Rotate map view
Ⓡ or Ⓡ	Change map viewing angle
BLK	Switch to/from top-down view
WHT	Skip turn

ARENA BATTLE CONTROLS (XBOX®)

Button	Command
Ⓛ	Movement
Ⓐ	Light melee attack
Ⓑ	Light magic attack
Ⓧ	Heavy melee attack
Ⓨ	Heavy magic attack
Ⓛ	Special magic attack
Ⓡ	Block
Ⓡ + Ⓛ	Strafe
START	Pause/resume

PlayStation®2

MENU CONTROLS (PS2)

Button	Command
Left analog stick	Highlight menu option
✕	Confirm selection
▲	Cancel selection/back up one menu

WORLD MAP CONTROLS (PS2)

Button	Command
Left analog stick/ directional buttons	Move cursor/highlight selection
✕	Confirm selection
▲	Cancel selection/command
■	Activate gate (when your selected character is on it)
L2 + ✕ or R2 + ✕	In-game help for selected tile
L1	Zoom out
R1	Zoom in
Right analog stick	Rotate map view/change map viewing angle
●	Switch to/from top-down view
SELECT	Skip turn

ARENA BATTLE CONTROLS (PS2)

Button	Command
Left analog stick	Movement
✕	Light melee attack
■	Light magic attack
●	Heavy melee attack
▲	Heavy magic attack
L1	Special magic attack
R1	Block
Left analog stick + R1	Strafe
START	Pause/resume

chapter 1
INTRODUCTION

Note
Arena Battle controls can be changed in the Options menu. The previous table lists the default controls.

IN-GAME HELP

Bring up the in-game Help menu to view a description of the currently selected tile's terrain.

While on the World Map, you can select a tile and press the Help button to view information about it, including its elemental alignment, terrain features, and an overview of the terrain. You can also scroll through other terrain types from this menu.

Press the Help Menu button while viewing terrain information to bring up the full Help menu.

Press the Help Menu button while viewing information about a tile, and you're taken to the in-game Help menu, which provides the following information:

Objectives: Conditions for victory on the current battle map and tips for achieving it.
Game Summary: An in-game version of the instruction manual, with information on the Battle arena and World Map interfaces and features.
Realms: Descriptions of the Light Order, Light Chaos, Dark Order, and Dark Chaos realms.
Creatures: Stats and abilities for every creature in the game.
Terrain: Information on the terrain tiles in the World Maps.
Structures: Details on the structures found on World Map tiles.
Spells: Descriptions, casting costs, and ranges for all magic spells.

GAME MODES
You can make five choices from the Main Menu: War Games, Versus, Team Fighter, Profiles, and Options.

War Games

The War Games menu includes the following options: Battle, Campaign, Tutorial, Load Game, and Army Builder.

wrath
unleashed
chapter 1

introduction
- welcome
- basic controls
- in-game help
- game modes

BATTLE

Battle mode lets you assemble a one- to one-player fight on a single World Map. For more information, refer to the "Battle Mode and Army Builder" section of this guide.

CAMPAIGN

Campaign mode is a series of 16 missions. A storyline runs through all of them. Completing missions unlocks hidden game features. Refer the "Campaign Mode" section of this guide for more info.

TUTORIAL

The Tutorial is an invaluable tool for quickly picking up the basics of *Wrath Unleashed*. Novice players should definitely run through it once before playing. Refer to "Getting Started" in this guide for more information on the Tutorial.

LOAD GAME

As the name implies, this menu option lets you load a saved game quickly and easily. The "Getting Started" section has more information on loading and saving game data.

ARMY BUILDER

Create and save custom Battle mode armies with the Army Builder. More information on the Army Builder can be found in the "Battle Mode and Army Builder" section of this guide.

Versus

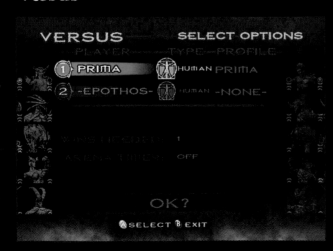

Versus mode is an arena combat-only game mode in which two creatures duke it out in a single fight, just like a standard fighting game. Refer to "Versus and Team Fighter Modes" for more information on setting up Versus mode battles.

Team Fighter

Team Fighter is an expanded version of Versus mode, in which each player picks a team of creatures that face off one-on-one until one team is defeated. See "Versus and Team Fighter Modes" for more details.

Profiles

Before you can play any *Wrath Unleashed* game modes, you need to create or load a profile, which stores information about your *WU* experiences. All the following Profiles menu options are explored in greater detail in the "Getting Started" section of this guide.

INTRODUCTION

NEW PROFILE

Use this option to create a new profile.

LOAD PROFILE

Load an existing profile with this menu option.

SAVE PROFILE

Wrath Unleashed automatically saves your game progress after you achieve an important accomplishment, but if you want to manually save your progress, use this option.

BATTLE RECORD

Select this option to view your combat record.

Options

The Options menu lets you customize different aspects of the game. Refer to the "Getting Started" section of this guide for more information.

CONTROLS

Change the default Battle arena button commands.

VIDEO

Change different aspects of the way the game is displayed on your television.

AUDIO

Raise or lower the volume for different sounds in the game.

BONUS FEATURES

Play demos or view unlocked Bonus Gallery artwork. See "Game Secrets" for more information on the Bonus Gallery artwork.

CREDITS

See the names of the fine folks who brought you *Wrath Unleashed*.

GETTING STARTED

PROFILES

The name of the profile you're currently using and saving game data to appears in the upper-left corner of the screen. If you have several saved profiles in the same location (because you're sharing *Wrath Unleashed* with another player, for instance), load your own profile before playing the game.

Create a Profile

wrath unleashed chapter 2

getting started
◆ *profiles*
◆ *game data*
◆ *game options*
◆ *tutorial mode*

Before you play any game mode in *Wrath Unleashed*, you must create a profile (or load a previously created profile). Your game progress and Battle record are automatically saved to your profile as you play. To create or load a profile, choose the Profiles option from the Main Menu.

Note

Game features that you unlock (Battle maps, campaign missions, etc.) are unlocked only in the currently loaded profile. If you want to use those game features, you must load the profile in which you unlocked them.

To start with a new profile, select "Create a Profile" from the Profiles menu, then choose where you want to save the profile (to a PS2 Memory Card, or the Xbox hard drive or memory unit).

Note

You can have up to four profiles saved in one location.

Select one of the four profile save slots; you can only create a profile in a slot labeled "- EMPTY -".

Finally, name the profile and choose "Done" to create it. Do not turn off your game console or remove the memory unit while the profile is saving. After the profile is saved, you automatically return to the Profiles menu.

The upper-left corner of the screen displays the active profile.

Save a Profile

Wrath Unleashed automatically saves your profile after you complete a battle or round of any game mode. To save your profile manually at any point in the game, choose "Save Profile" from the Profiles menu, and the currently loaded profile will save.

Load a Profile

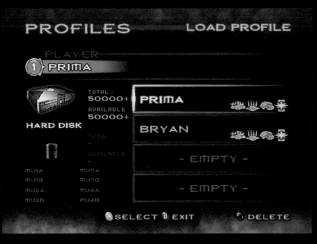

To continue saving progress to an existing profile, and to use the game features you've unlocked in that profile, load it by selecting "Load Profile" from the Profiles menu. Choose the location where the profile is saved, then select the name of the saved profile from the list of profiles that appears.

Delete a Profile

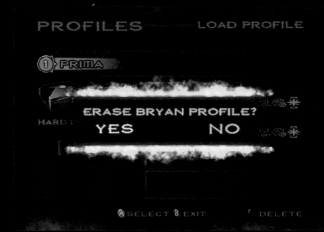

To delete a saved profile, select "Create a Profile" or "Save a Profile" from the Profiles menu and choose the location of the profile you wish to delete. When the list of saved profiles appears, highlight the one you want to erase and press "Delete" (in the lower-right corner of the screen) to delete the profile.

Caution
After you confirm your decision to delete a profile, that profile is erased from your console and can never be recovered. Be sure you want to delete the profile before doing this.

PRIMA'S OFFICIAL STRATEGY GUIDE

Battle Record

getting started
- *profiles*
- *game data*
- *game options*
- *tutorial mode*

If you have loaded a profile, you can choose to view your Battle record in that profile by choosing "Battle Record" from the Profiles menu. The Battle Record menu has three options: War Data, Arena Data, and Medals.

WAR DATA
War Data lists the wins, losses, and win percentage for the four factions (Light Order, Dark Order, Light Chaos, and Dark Chaos). It shows how well each faction has performed on the battlefield under your command.

ARENA DATA
Arena Data shows how well each creature type has fared on the battlefield under your control. As with War Data, Arena Data shows the wins, losses, and win percentage for each creature you've commanded in any arena battle in any game mode.

MEDALS
You can earn eight medals in *Wrath Unleashed*. Each represents a specific accomplishment. To see which you've unlocked, which you have yet to earn, and how to get them, choose "Medals" from the Battle Record menu.

Note
Unlocking medals doesn't unlock other game features, but you unlock game features as you unlock medals. For instance, to earn the Light Order Campaign medal, you must complete all Light Order Missions in Campaign mode, which also unlocks the Light Order God, four Bonus Gallery images, and the two-player map, Red 5. Refer to "Game Secrets" at the end of this guide for more information on hidden game features.

CONDITIONS FOR EARNING MEDALS

NAME:
LIGHT ORDER CAMPAIGN

CONDITION:
Complete all Light Order Campaign Missions

NAME:
LIGHT CHAOS CAMPAIGN

CONDITION:
Complete all Light Chaos Campaign Missions

NAME:
DARK ORDER CAMPAIGN

CONDITION:
Complete all Dark Order Campaign Missions

NAME:
DARK CHAOS CAMPAIGN

CONDITION:
Complete all Dark Chaos Campaign Missions

GETTING STARTED

NAME:
REALM MASTER

CONDITION:
Complete all 16
Campaign Missions

NAME:
STRATEGIST

CONDITION:
Win 20 Battle mode
games

NAME:
TACTICIAN

CONDITION:
Win 20 Team Fighter
matches

NAME:
DEFENDER

CONDITION:
Win 100 Battle Arena
matches

GAME DATA
As long as you have loaded a profile, your game data is automatically saved to the profile after you complete any game mode. You can also save the game data manually.

Auto-Saving Game Data

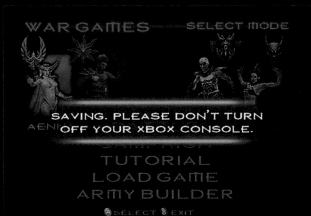

Your profile data is automatically saved.

Wrath Unleashed saves your profile data after you win or lose an arena battle or World Map war in any game mode. The auto-saving feature is designed to record your win/loss progress for the purposes of unlocking hidden game features. You don't have to do anything except play through the game to save this data.

Caution
When *Wrath Unleashed* is saving your profile data, a message appears on the screen telling you not to turn off the power to your console or remove the memory unit to which the data is being saved. As long as you follow these instructions, you won't have any trouble with your profile data.

Manually Saving Game Data

PAUSE   SELECT OPTION

PLAYER
1 PRIMA

RESUME
SAVE GAME
OPTIONS
QUIT

A SELECT B EXIT

Choose "Save Game" from the in-game Pause menu to resume your progress in that game at a later time.

If you need to stop playing *Wrath Unleashed* halfway through a Campaign Mission or Battle mode war, choose "Save Game" from the Pause menu to record your game progress.

You can then resume the game at that point any time by choosing "Load Game" from the War Games menu.

PRIMA'S OFFICIAL STRATEGY GUIDE

GAME OPTIONS

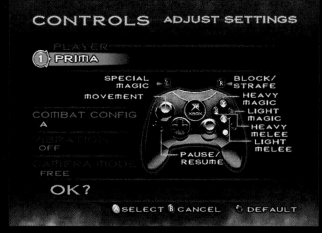

OPTIONS   SELECT OPTION

PLAYER
1 PRIMA

CONTROLS
VIDEO
AUDIO
BONUS FEATURES
CREDITS

SELECT   EXIT

Selecting "Options" from the Main Menu brings up the Options menu, which has five sub-menus: Controls, Video, Audio, Bonus Features, and Credits. Changes made to the default options are automatically saved to your profile.

Controls

CONTROLS   ADJUST SETTINGS

PLAYER
1 PRIMA

SPECIAL MAGIC   BLOCK/STRAFE
MOVEMENT   HEAVY MAGIC
COMBAT CONFIG A   LIGHT MAGIC
  HEAVY MELEE
VIBRATION OFF   LIGHT MELEE
CAMERA MODE FREE   PAUSE/RESUME

OK?

SELECT   CANCEL   DEFAULT

The Controls menu allows you to customize your *Wrath Unleashed* controls.

CONTROLS MENU OPTIONS

OPTION	DESCRIPTION
Combat Config	Change the default arena combat controls.
Vibration	Turn the controller's vibration function on or off.
Camera Mode	Switch between a Free or Preset (fixed) camera.

Video

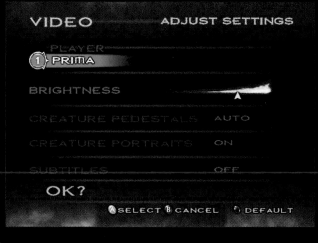

VIDEO   ADJUST SETTINGS

PLAYER
1 PRIMA

BRIGHTNESS

CREATURE PEDESTALS   AUTO

CREATURE PORTRAITS   ON

SUBTITLES   OFF

OK?

SELECT   CANCEL   DEFAULT

Use the Video menu options to change how *Wrath Unleashed* is displayed on your TV.

VIDEO MENU OPTIONS

OPTION	DESCRIPTION
Brightness	Set the brightness level for the game.
Creature Pedestals	Turn World Map creature pedestals on or off; "Auto" lets the game choose whether they should be displayed.
Creature Portraits	Turn portraits of the creatures on or off during gameplay.
Subtitles	View (on) or hide (off) subtitles during cinematic sequences.

Audio

The Audio menu lets you set the volume levels of three different sets of game sounds: Effects, Music, and Speech. Use your TV volume to set the overall volume level.

AUDIO MENU OPTIONS

OPTION	DESCRIPTION
Effects Volume	Set the volume level of the sound effects.
Music Volume	Set the volume level of the background music.
Speech Volume	Set the volume level of the spoken dialogue during cinematic sequences.

Bonus Features

From the Bonus Features menu, you can choose to view the Bonus Gallery or play demos of upcoming LucasArts games.

BONUS GALLERY

Playing through *Wrath Unleashed*'s Campaign mode unlocks 16 pieces of concept art in the Bonus Gallery.

BONUS GALLERY UNLOCKING CONDITIONS

IMAGES	CONDITIONS
Two Light Order images	Complete Light Order Mission #1.
Two additional Light Order images	Complete Light Order Mission #3.
Two Dark Order images	Complete Dark Order Mission #1.
Two additional Dark Order images	Complete Dark Order Mission #3.
Two Light Chaos images	Complete Light Chaos Mission #1.
Two additional Light Chaos images	Complete Light Chaos Mission #3.
Two Dark Chaos images	Complete Dark Chaos Mission #1.
Two additional Dark Chaos images	Complete Dark Chaos Mission #3.

Credits

Select "Credits" from the Options menu to view the game credits.

TUTORIAL MODE

getting
started
◆ profiles
◆ game data
◆ game options
◆ tutorial mode

Select "Tutorial" from the War Games menu to begin Tutorial mode.

Choose "Tutorial" from the War Games menu to begin the Tutorial mode, a short interactive guide that brings novice players up to speed on how to play *Wrath Unleashed*. Tutorial mode is summarized here, but there's no substitute for playing through it. Run through Tutorial mode once before playing *Wrath Unleashed*.

Overview

Each game's overview lists the objectives for the game.

Tutorial mode begins with an overview, like every other Campaign or Battle mode game. The World Map appears in the screen's upper-left corner, and the game objectives appear in the center.

At the screen's bottom are two options: Start Game and Briefing. Start Game begins the Tutorial. Briefing gives you additional information

about the upcoming game, which appears in the screen's upper-right corner.

Prepare for battle!

After choosing "Start Game," you see a loading screen that shows the rival Overlords who command each opposing army. For the purposes of the Tutorial, you command the Light Order army, which has the water-aligned Aenna as its Overlord. For more information on the various armies and Overlords, see the next section of this guide, "Overlords and Creatures."

Viewing the World Map

You see the World Map from a God's-eye view.

In Tutorial mode, you learn first how to use the controls that allow you to view the World Map from a variety of angles.

Note

Commands for changing the World Map view differ depending on which console you're playing. Refer to the instructions in the screen's upper-right corner or the "Introduction" section of this guide for a list of your console's controls.

GETTING STARTED

In this section of the Tutorial, you:

◆ Rotate your view of the World Map.
◆ Change the angle of view of the World Map.
◆ Zoom in and out on the World Map.
◆ Toggle between top-down and 3D views of the World Map.

After you perform each of these tasks, following the onscreen instructions, continue to the next section of the Tutorial.

Selecting and Moving Creatures

Highlight a creature with the cursor and select it.

The next lessons in the Tutorial involve selecting and moving your army's creatures. The Tutorial requires you to move your Light Order Centaur, so move the cursor to the tile the Centaur stands on (marked with a green arrow) and select the Centaur.

Several adjacent tiles are outlined in yellow, representing your Centaur's movement range. You can move your Centaur to any tile within the yellow outline.

TERRAIN TYPES
Terrain types are displayed at the bottom of the screen. A tile's terrain type determines which creatures have advantages when battling on that tile. For instance, Light Order creatures (who are aligned with water) have an advantage on water-aligned terrains, such as glaciers, seas, and swamps.

Move your Centaur onto the highlighted plains terrain and confirm your decision to proceed to the next step of the Tutorial.

Moving Different Creatures

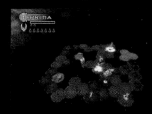

When you move your Centaur, more of your creatures appear on the World Map.

More tiles and creatures appear after you move your Centaur to the plains tile. Move the cursor over each to view the creature's name, rank, portrait, and health.

Now you learn how to move different types of creatures. Each creature in your army moves by one of three methods: walking, teleporting, and flying.

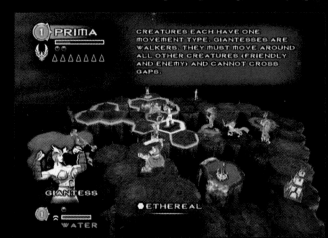

Walkers, such as the Giantess, can't cross gaps or tiles occupied by other creatures.

Fliers, like your Frost Dragon, can cross spaces occupied by other creatures but cannot cross gaps.

Teleporters, like this Unicorn, have the most versatile movement type; they can cross gaps and spaces occupied by other creatures.

MORE ON TERRAIN TYPES

After you move your Giantess, Unicorn, and Frost Dragon, the Tutorial mode tells you more about terrain types. Not only should you stay on terrains that favor your water-aligned Light Order army (glacier, sea, swamp), but you should also avoid placing your creatures on tiles that favor your fire-aligned Light Chaos adversary (mountains, lava, and desert).

To conclude this part of the Tutorial, find and select your Genie, who is on a lava tile, and move it to the nearby dead terrain, which does not favor your Light Chaos adversary.

Battling Enemy Creatures

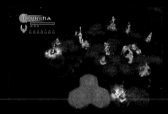

After you move your Genie, enemy creatures appear:

Now that you've learned how to move your own creatures and position them strategically, it's time to do battle with the enemy. After you move your Genie, a few Light Chaos creatures appear.

Battles can be won or lost before they even start; your success depends upon how carefully you choose your battles. Fight on terrain that favors your creatures, not the enemy's.

FIRST BATTLE

Battle #1: Centaur vs. Unicorn on ethereal terrain.

Your first battle pits your Centaur against the enemy Light Chaos Unicorn on the ethereal terrain next to the Centaur. Ethereal terrain doesn't provide an advantage to either creature, so it's a fair fight.

This is also your first glimpse of arena combat, where *Wrath Unleashed* armies' creatures clash. Use your various attacks to whittle down the Unicorn's health and win the battle (refer to the "Introduction" section of this guide for your console's arena combat controls).

Note

You can't lose this fight. If your Centaur's health is depleted, the game refills it and sends you back for more punishment. Don't expect this kind of treatment outside of the Tutorial mode!

The fight analysis screen appears after combat ends.

After the fight is over, the fight analysis screen appears. It shows who won, how much health each creature lost, how successful their melee and magic attacks were, and how much health (if any) each creature has left.

CAPTURING STRUCTURES

The Centaur gains possession of the Temple the Unicorn defended.

After you defeat the enemy Unicorn, you also gain possession of the Temple on the tile the Unicorn was defending. Capturing structures on tiles gives you various advantages in *Wrath Unleashed* (see the "World Maps" section of this guide for more information on structures).

A structure belongs to the army whose creature occupies the tile on which it stands. If a structure stands on a tile that has no creature on it, the structure can be captured by the army that moves a creature onto it. Move your Giantess onto the unoccupied Temple nearby to capture it and proceed to the next part of the Tutorial.

Several World Maps require you to capture a certain number of structures to win. Temples are worth one point; Citadels are worth two points. Your total appears in the upper-left corner of the screen as a series of filled-in triangles.

MANA AND SPELLS

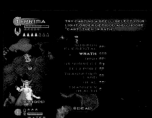

Capturing structures increases your Mana flow, which lets you cast powerful spells more frequently.

After each round of the game, your army generates Mana, if your army has a creature standing on a temple, citadel, or Mana wat–the more creatures, the more Mana, which you can use to cast spells. Your Mana is displayed in the upper-left corner of the screen as a purple bar and a series of purple orbs. Each time the purple bar is filled, another half-orb appears under it. The more powerful the spell, the more Mana it costs to cast.

Only Adepts, Demigods, and Gods can cast spells, and Demigods and Gods have access to the spells Wrath and Resurrect, which Adepts cannot cast. When any unit stands on a magic amplifier (which is in some maps), it can then cast adept-level spells–but not Resurrect or Wrath. The next step of the Tutorial requires you to select your Demigod Overlord, choose "Cast" from the menu that appears, and fry a nearby enemy Unicorn with the Wrath spell, which costs three Mana orbs to cast. Because the Unicorn is a weak creature, the Wrath spell obliterates it.

SECOND BATTLE

Move to the last Light Chaos Unicorn and attack it on the next turn.

The final battle in Tutorial mode requires you to take out the last Light Chaos Unicorn, who occupies a Temple. The Temple protects the Unicorn from magical attack, so you can't just hit it with another Wrath spell.

The Unicorn is also of Sentinel rank, which means that you can't attack it with a creature unless the creature started its turn adjacent to the Unicorn. That means that attacking the Unicorn is a two-turn process. First, move your nearby Juggernaut next to the Unicorn. On the next turn, move the Juggernaut onto the Unicorn's tile and do battle.

Victory is yours!

After you defeat the Unicorn (which shouldn't be a challenge, as the Juggernaut is much more powerful), you have successfully completed Tutorial mode.

Note

Between this section of the guide and the "Introduction" section, you should now have a basic understanding of how to play *Wrath Unleashed*. But there's a lot more to learn, so check out the rest of the guide for more detailed and advanced techniques.

OVERLORDS & CREATURES

LIGHT ⊙ ORDER

overlords
& creatures
◆ light order
◆ light chaos
◆ dark order
◆ dark chaos

LIGHT ORDER CREATURES AT A GLANCE

Name	Rank	Health Orbs*	Magic Orbs*	Movement Range	Movement Type**	Army Builder Cost	Team Fighter Cost	Resurrect Cost***
Centaur	Sentinel	1	1	3	Walker	1	1	1.5
Unicorn	Sentinel	1	1	2	Teleporter	1	1	1.5
Giantess	Warrior	2	1	4	Walker	2	2	
Genie	Warrior	2	1	3	Flyer	2	2	3
Water Elemental	Warrior	2	2	Summon Only	Summon Only	n/a	3	2. (Summon)
Juggernaut Adept	Champion	3	2	5	Walker	6	4	4.5
Frost Dragon	Champion	3	2	5	Flyer	5	4	4.5
Ogre Mage	Champion	3	2	5	Walker	4	4	4.5
Demigod	Overlord	4	3	5	Walker	8	8	n/a
God	Overlord	5	3	5	Flyer	12	10	n/a

* *Health orbs* and *magic orbs* in the table also include the full bar of health or magic energy the creature starts out with.
** *Movement type* indicates what terrain the creature can cross. *Teleporters* can cross gaps and tiles occupied by other creatures. *Flyers* can cross tiles occupied by other creatures but cannot cross gaps. *Walkers* can't cross gaps or tiles occupied by other creatures.
*** *Resurrect cost* is the number of Mana orbs required to resurrect the creature.

OVERLORDS & CREATURES

CENTAUR

Centaurs are efficient, low-cost creatures with a variety of uses. Their Sentinel Barrier ability makes them excellent Temple guardians, and their speed and variety of attacks serve them well in arena combat. Although they're often overwhelmed when facing more powerful creatures in combat, a skilled player uses the Centaur's quickness to get in a couple of hits on an adversary and then backs off before the Centaurs suffer a counterattack.

Tip

Press the attack constantly when controlling a Light Order Centaur. Its signature attack is activated when dashing toward an enemy, and its magic and melee attacks are designed to inflict as much punishment as possible in the shortest amount of time.

Rank: Sentinel
Health Energy: 1
Magic Energy: 1
Movement Range: 3 tiles

Movement Type: Walker
Army Builder Cost: 1
Team Fighter Cost: 1
Resurrect Cost: 1.5

CENTAUR MOVE LIST

Attack	Name
Light Melee	Quick Axe Slash
Heavy Melee	Heavy Axe Slash
Light Magic	Throw Weapon
Heavy Magic	Trap
Special Magic	Ram Attack
Signature Attack	Back Kick (LLLH while running)

Note

Centaurs, like all Sentinels, have the Sentinel Barrier ability, which means they can't be attacked by creatures unless those creatures began their turns on a tile adjacent to the Centaur. Also, creatures can't move past Centaurs unless they defeat the Centaurs in combat.

Throw Weapon

Back Kick (Part 1)

Trap

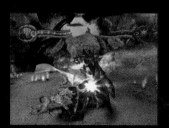

Back Kick (Part 2)

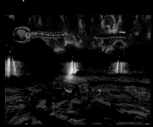

Ram Attack

Back Kick (Part 3)

UNICORN

Unicorns are best used to quickly capture Temples and other structures of strategic importance on the World Map. They are the only Light Order creatures with the innate ability to teleport across narrow gaps in the World Map, and their Sentinel Barrier ability helps protect them from attack. In arena combat, Unicorns aren't as fast or powerful as Centaurs, but their versatility on the World Map helps make up for that.

Tip

If your opponent has you backed into a corner, use the Blink ability to teleport to another part of the arena. If you manage to reappear on top of your opponent, you can inflict some serious damage.

*wrath
unleashed
chapter 3*

**overlords
& creatures**
- *light order*
- *light chaos*
- *dark order*
- *dark chaos*

Rank: Sentinel
Health Energy: 1
Magic Energy: 1
Movement Range: 2 tiles

Movement Type: Teleporter
Army Builder Cost: 1
Team Fighter Cost: 1
Resurrect Cost: 1.5

UNICORN MOVE LIST

Attack	Name
Light Melee	Horn Jab
Heavy Melee	Horn Slice
Light Magic	Throw Weapon
Heavy Magic	Magic Blast
Special Magic	Blink
Signature Attack	Mystic Hoof Stomp (LLHH)

Note

Unicorns, like all Sentinels, have the Sentinel Barrier ability, which means they can't be attacked by creatures unless those creatures began their turns on a tile adjacent to the Unicorn. Also, creatures can't move past Unicorns unless they defeat the Unicorns in combat.

Throw Weapon

Mystic Hoof Stomp (Part 1)

Magic Blast

Mystic Hoof Stomp (Part 2)

Blink

Mystic Hoof Stomp (Part 3)

GIANTESS

Giantesses pack a lot of power into a relatively low-cost package, but their impressive strength is countered by their slow attack speed. A quick enemy can get in close, unleash a combo of moves, and get back out before the Giantess has much chance to retaliate. However, the Giantess also has an impressive reach with that hammer of hers. Use it to your advantage and attack a bit more quickly than you would with other creatures.

Tip
A Giantess's Heal ability is helpful in battle. Hold down the Special Magic button to convert her magic energy into health energy. Try it while standing next to an Energy Crystal (especially after you've stunned or knocked your opponent with a Hammer Sweep). We recommend using the Heal ability near the end of a fight that you've almost won, so your Giantess is ready for the next scrap.

Rank: Warrior
Health Energy: 2
Magic Energy: 1
Movement Range: 4 tiles

Movement Type: Walker
Army Builder Cost: 2
Team Fighter Cost: 2
Resurrect Cost: 3

Hammer Crush

Hammer Sweep (Part 1)

Stun Horn

Hammer Sweep (Part 2)

Heal

Hammer Sweep (Part 3)

GIANTESS MOVE LIST

Attack	Name
Light Melee	Light Hammer Swing
Heavy Melee	Heavy Hammer Swing
Light Magic	Hammer Crush
Heavy Magic	Stun Horn
Special Magic	Heal
Signature Attack	Hammer Sweep (LLLH)

GENIE

If there's one word to describe Genies, it's "fast." Their flying ability lets them move quickly around the World Map, and their lightning quickness in arena combat can send even more formidable enemies to defeat. Genies are especially vicious with attack combos, chaining together staff hits with ease. Add in the ability to Blink (teleport) around the arena, and you have a fight on your hands whenever you face one of these creatures.

Tip

The Genie's Grab & Throw ability levitates nearby neutral terrain features, such as boulders and rocks, and sends them flying at enemies. You can only use this ability when you're near something that can be thrown, but it's one of the best long-distance attacks in the game!

wrath unleashed chapter 3

overlords & creatures
- *light order*
- *light chaos*
- *dark order*
- *dark chaos*

Rank: Warrior	Movement Type: Flyer
Health Energy: 2	Army Builder Cost: 2
Magic Energy: 1	Team Fighter Cost: 2
Movement Range: 3 tiles	Resurrect Cost: 3

GENIE MOVE LIST

Attack	Name
Light Melee	Staff Jab
Heavy Melee	Staff Thrust
Light Magic	Magic Orb
Heavy Magic	Grab & Throw
Special Magic	Blink
Signature Attack	Whirling Blade (LLHH while running)

Magic Orb

Whirling Blade (Part 1)

Grab & Throw

Whirling Blade (Part 2)

Blink

Whirling Blade (Part 3)

WATER ELEMENTAL

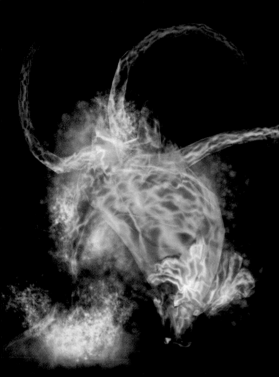

Water Elementals only appear in Battle and Campaign games when a Light Order creature casts Summon Elemental. Water Elementals must be summoned directly into combat with an enemy creature, and they vanish after the fight is over, regardless of who won. Water Elementals are fast, with an excellent attack range, and they are generally more powerful than any other Light Order creature of Warrior rank.

Tip

The Water Elemental's Dive ability is similar to the Blink ability used by Unicorns. Hold down the Special Magic button to cause the Water Elemental to dive into the ground; release the button to pop out. If you can move under an enemy before jumping out of the ground, you can inflict respectable damage. The longer you stay underground, the more magic energy you use.

Rank: Warrior
Health Energy: 2
Magic Energy: 2
Movement Range:
Summon Only

Movement Type:
Summon Only
Army Builder Cost: n/a
Team Fighter Cost: 3
Resurrect Cost: 2.5
(Summon Elemental Spell)

WATER ELEMENTAL MOVE LIST

Attack	Name
Light Melee	Quick Jab
Heavy Melee	Ranged Strike
Light Magic	Magic Beam
Heavy Magic	Magic Blast
Special Magic	Dive
Signature Attack	Impact Wave (LLLH)

Magic Beam

Impact Wave (Part 1)

Magic Blast

Impact Wave (Part 2)

Dive

Impact Wave (Part 3)

JUGGERNAUT ADEPT

wrath
unleashed
chapter 3

overlords
& creatures
◆ *light order*
◆ *light chaos*
◆ *dark order*
◆ *dark chaos*

For a spell-casting creature, the Juggernaut Adept also displays a remarkable degree of physical power. It is slow and lumbering, but its melee attacks inflict great damage, even though they're hard to combo together initially. It shares with the Genie the Grab & Throw ability, which allows it to magically pick up nearby rocks and hurl them across the arena to hit an enemy. Finally, the Force Sword signature attack lets the Juggernaut Adept knock an opponent for a loop and set them up for a follow-up attack.

Tip

When fighting a Juggernaut Adept, watch out for the Ram attack! It's easy to dodge if you've kept enough distance from the beast, as the attack sends the Juggernaut Adept in a straight line. If you get caught by a Ram attack, you suffer a frightening amount of damage.

Rank: Champion	Movement Type: Walker
Health Energy: 3	Army Builder Cost: 6
Magic Energy: 2	Team Fighter Cost: 4
Movement Range: 5 tiles	Resurrect Cost: 4.5

JUGGERNAUT ADEPT MOVE LIST

Attack	Name
Light Melee	Head Jab
Heavy Melee	Spinning Head Thrust
Light Magic	Magic Orb
Heavy Magic	Grab & Throw
Special Magic	Ram Attack
Signature Attack	Force Sword (LLLH)

Magic Orb

Force Sword (Part 1)

Grab & Throw

Force Sword (Part 2)

Ram Attack

Force Sword (Part 3)

FROST DRAGON

Frost Dragons are quick for their size, which an unwary opponent learns the hard way. Their melee attacks chain together nicely into combos, and they can zip around World Maps and Battle arenas with equal ease. The Frost Dragon's Breath attack is formidable, but is also the beast's slowest attack. It is easy to dodge the brunt of the blast.

Tip
The Frost Dragon's size is its biggest disadvantage. If you can attack a Frost Dragon from the side or from behind, you can do a lot of damage before it can back off, turn around, and defend itself.

Rank: Champion	Movement Type: Flyer
Health Energy: 3	Army Builder Cost: 5
Magic Energy: 2	Team Fighter Cost: 4
Movement Range: 5 tiles	Resurrect Cost: 4.5

FROST DRAGON MOVE LIST

Attack	Name
Light Melee	Claw Swipe
Heavy Melee	Claw Thrust
Light Magic	Magic Orb
Heavy Magic	Breath
Special Magic	Dive
Signature Attack	Tunneling Tail (LLLH while running)

Magic Orb

Tunneling Tail (Part 1)

Breath

Tunneling Tail (Part 2)

Dive

Tunneling Tail (Part 3)

OGRE MAGE

wrath unleashed chapter 3

overlords & creatures

◆ *light order*
◆ *light chaos*
◆ *dark order*
◆ *dark chaos*

Ogre Mages are big, violent bruisers that blend powerful magical attacks with crushing physical assaults. Like Genies, Ogre Mages can chain together combinations of heavy and light melee attacks to whittle an opponent down to size quickly. The only drawback that an Ogre Mage suffers from in arena combat is its slow attack speed. It is also limited on the World Map by the fact that it's a walker, but its generous movement range helps make up for that.

Tip
Don't overlook the Ogre Mage's magical versatility in combat. Use the Magic Orb to freeze opponents solid and set them up for heavy melee strikes. At close range, Trap is a brutal attack, and the Ogre Mage's Magic Shield is the ultimate defense against virtually any magic attack.

Rank: Champion	Movement Type: Walker
Health Energy: 3	Army Builder Cost: 4
Magic Energy: 2	Team Fighter Cost: 4
Movement Range: 5 tiles	Resurrect Cost: 4.5

OGRE MAGE MOVE LIST

Attack	Name
Light Melee	Quick Sword Slash
Heavy Melee	Heavy Sword Slash
Light Magic	Magic Orb
Heavy Magic	Trap
Special Magic	Magic Shield
Signature Attack	Phantom Blade (LLHH)

Magic Orb

Phantom Blade (Part 1)

Trap

Phantom Blade (Part 2)

Magic Shield

Phantom Blade (Part 3)

DEMIGOD

In her Demigod form, Aenna is more than a match for any non-Overlord creature foolish enough to confront her. This placid goddess of the water displays a tsunami-like wrath in battle, effortlessly chaining together combos of melee attacks. Her Magic Shield protects her against a foe's magical attacks, and repeated use of her Magic Beam can keep enemy creatures at a distance.

Tip
Although Aenna is a powerful warrior, don't put her on the front lines of combat too often in Battle or Campaign games. If Aenna is killed in arena combat, you lose the game.

Rank: Overlord	Movement Type: Walker
Health Energy: 4	Army Builder Cost: 8
Magic Energy: 3	Team Fighter Cost: 8
Movement Range: 5 tiles	Resurrect Cost: n/a

DEMIGOD MOVE LIST

Attack	Name
Light Melee	Light Bolt
Heavy Melee	Heavy Bolt
Light Magic	Magic Beam
Heavy Magic	Magic Blast
Special Magic	Magic Shield
Signature Attack	Ice Wall (LLLH while running)

Magic Beam

Ice Wall (Part 1)

Magic Blast

Ice Wall (Part 2)

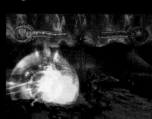

Magic Shield

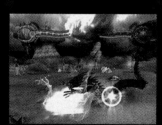

Ice Wall (Part 3)

PRIMA'S OFFICIAL STRATEGY GUIDE

*overlords
& creatures*

◆ *light order*
◆ *light chaos*
◆ *dark order*
◆ *dark chaos*

GOD

Aenna's God form is the most powerful Light Order creature in *Wrath Unleashed*. Her melee attacks are largely unchanged, but her magical attacks are greatly increased. The Ethereal Purge ability takes a few seconds to execute, and Aenna is vulnerable to attack while casting it, but if it is successful, it inflicts a tremendous amount of damage on an adversary. Cast Ethereal Purge at a distance from your enemy; it strikes them unerringly, no matter how they try to dodge.

Tip

Learn the God signature attack, Energy Nova, as soon as possible. It's the most deadly move in Aenna's arsenal. If it connects, it can do almost a full bar's worth of damage to an adversary. If you're fighting Aenna and see her float up into the air and vanish in a flash of light, get ready to block!

Magic Beam

Energy Nova (Part 1)

Ethereal Purge

Energy Nova (Part 2)

Rank: Overlord	Movement Type: Flyer
Health Energy: 5	Army Builder Cost: 12
Magic Energy: 5	Team Fighter Cost: 10
Movement Range: 5 tiles	Resurrect Cost: n/a

GOD MOVE LIST

Attack	Name
Light Melee	Light Bolt
Heavy Melee	Heavy Bolt
Light Magic	Magic Beam
Heavy Magic	Ethereal Purge
Special Magic	Magic Shield
Signature Attack	Energy Nova (LLLH while running)

Magic Shield

Energy Nova (Part 3)

OVERLORDS & CREATURES

LIGHT CHAOS

LIGHT CHAOS CREATURES AT A GLANCE

Name	Rank	Health Orbs*	Magic Orbs*	Movement Range	Movement Type**	Army Builder Cost	Team Fighter Cost	Resurrect Cost***
Centaur	Sentinel	1	1	3	Walker	1	1	1.5
Unicorn	Sentinel	1	1	2	Teleporter	1	1	1.5
Giantess	Warrior	2	1	4	Walker	2	2	3
Genie	Warrior	2	1	3	Flyer	2	2	3
Fire Elemental	Warrior	2	2	Summon Only	Summon Only	n/a	3	2.5 (Summon)
Juggernaut Adept	Champion	3	2	5	Walker	6	4	4.5
Blaze Dragon	Champion	3	2	5	Flyer	5	4	4.5
Fire Giant	Champion	3	2	5	Walker	4	4	4.5
Demigod	Overlord	4	3	5	Walker	8	8	n/a
God	Overlord	5	3	5	Flyer	12	10	n/a

* *Health orbs* and *magic orbs* in the table also include the full bar of health or magic energy the creature starts out with.

** *Movement type* indicates what terrain the creature can cross. *Teleporters* can cross gaps and tiles occupied by other creatures. *Flyers* can cross tiles occupied by other creatures but cannot cross gaps. *Walkers* can't cross gaps or tiles occupied by other creatures.

*** *Resurrect cost* is the number of Mana orbs required to resurrect the creature.

PRIMA'S OFFICIAL STRATEGY GUIDE

CENTAUR

If you think of *Wrath Unleashed* as a game of chess, Centaurs are your pawns. They're best used to conquer unoccupied structures and to act as Sentinel Barriers to keep enemy creatures from marching through your territory. They're also impressive in combat, with excellent long-range attacks (Throw Weapon, Ram attack) and some good, quick melee attacks that can be combined into fierce combo attacks.

wrath unleashed chapter 3

overlords & creatures

- *light order*
- *light chaos*
- *dark order*
- *dark chaos*

Tip

When fighting a larger creature with a Centaur, use the Centaur's natural speed to your advantage. Hit your enemy with a quick LLH combo and back off. If you get a chance to use the Back Kick, you inflict a great deal of damage in a short amount of time.

Rank: Sentinel	Movement Type: Walker
Health Energy: 1	Army Builder Cost: 1
Magic Energy: 1	Team Fighter Cost: 1
Movement Range: 3 tiles	Resurrect Cost: 1.5

Throw Weapon

Back Kick (Part 1)

CENTAUR MOVE LIST

Attack	Name
Light Melee	Quick Axe Slash
Heavy Melee	Heavy Axe Slash
Light Magic	Throw Weapon
Heavy Magic	Trap
Special Magic	Ram Attack
Signature Attack	Back Kick (LLLH while running)

Trap

Back Kick (Part 2)

Note

Centaurs, like all Sentinels, have the Sentinel Barrier ability, which means they can't be attacked by creatures unless those creatures began their turns on a tile adjacent to the Centaur. Also, creatures can't move past Centaurs unless they defeat the Centaurs in combat.

Ram Attack

Back Kick (Part 3)

OVERLORDS & CREATURES

UNICORN

Unicorns are possibly the least impressive Light Chaos creatures when it comes to arena combat–they suffer from a lack of health and magic energy, and their attacks aren't as fast or powerful as a Centaur's. However, Unicorns are the only Light Chaos creatures that can teleport, which allows them to capture unoccupied Temples and other structures on the other side of gaps in the World Map. You can also use their Sentinel Barrier ability to slow the advance of enemy forces.

Tip

When using a Unicorn in arena combat, stay at a distance from your opponent and zap your adversary with the Throw Weapon attack as many times as possible. In close-quarters combat, work the LLH and LLLH combinations.

Rank: Sentinel
Health Energy: 1
Magic Energy: 1
Movement Range: 2 tiles

Movement Type: Teleporter
Army Builder Cost: 1
Team Fighter Cost: 1
Resurrect Cost: 1.5

UNICORN MOVE LIST

Attack	Name
Light Melee	Horn Jab
Heavy Melee	Horn Slice
Light Magic	Throw Weapon
Heavy Magic	Magic Blast
Special Magic	Blink
Signature Attack	Mystic Hoof Stomp (LLHH)

Throw Weapon

Mystic Hoof Stomp (Part 1)

Magic Blast

Mystic Hoof Stomp (Part 2)

Note

Unicorns, like all Sentinels, have the Sentinel Barrier ability, which means they can't be attacked by creatures unless those creatures began their turns on a tile adjacent to the Unicorn. Also, creatures can't move past Unicorns unless they defeat the Unicorns in combat.

Blink

Mystic Hoof Stomp (Part 3)

GIANTESS

Giantesses are the most physically powerful Light Chaos Warriors (other than Fire Elementals). They carry enormous mallets that give them melee attacks of above-average range and power. However, they're also the slowest Light Chaos Warriors; a lighter, faster foe can usually get a few hits in before the Giantess can swing her hammer.

wrath
unleashed
chapter 3

overlords
& creatures
◆ light order
◆ light chaos
◆ dark order
◆ dark chaos

Tip
Don't overlook the Giantess's Heal ability. Hold in the Special Magic button to transform magic energy into health energy. Use this ability just before winning a battle, and your Giantess starts the next fight refreshed and ready to rumble.

Hammer Crush

Hammer Sweep (Part 1)

Stun Horn

Hammer Sweep (Part 2)

Heal

Hammer Sweep (Part 3)

Rank: Warrior	Movement Type: Walker
Health Energy: 1	Army Builder Cost: 2
Magic Energy: 1	Team Fighter Cost: 2
Movement Range: 4 tiles	Resurrect Cost: 3

GIANTESS MOVE LIST

Attack	Name
Light Melee	Light Hammer Swing
Heavy Melee	Heavy Hammer Swing
Light Magic	Hammer Crush
Heavy Magic	Stun Horn
Special Magic	Heal
Signature Attack	Hammer Sweep (LLLH while running)

OVERLORDS & CREATURES

GENIE

A Genie's greatest asset is its terrific speed. It can chain together combinations of melee attacks until a foe lies battered and broken on the arena floor, and it's also quite spry in strafing and dodging enemy attacks. Thanks to their flying ability, Genies can also move around the World Map relatively unimpeded. Use your Sentinels to seize unoccupied structures; use Genies to take Temples that are guarded by enemy creatures.

Tip
In addition to their impressive melee combat abilities, Genies can also obliterate enemies from a distance. Use Fireballs to soften up a foe at the start of a fight, and cast Grab & Throw near boulders to hurl them unerringly at your enemy.

Rank: Warrior	Movement Type: Flyer
Health Energy: 2	Army Builder Cost: 2
Magic Energy: 1	Team Fighter Cost: 2
Movement Range: 3 tiles	Resurrect Cost: 3

GENIE MOVE LIST

Attack	Name
Light Melee	Staff Jab
Heavy Melee	Staff Thrust
Light Magic	Fireball
Heavy Magic	Grab & Throw
Special Magic	Blink
Signature Attack	1000 Whirlwinds (LLLH)

Fireball

1000 Whirlwinds (Part 1)

Grab & Throw

1000 Whirlwinds (Part 2)

Blink

1000 Whirlwinds (Part 3)

FIRE ELEMENTAL

*wrath
unleashed
chapter 3*

**overlords
& creatures**
◆ *light order*
◆ *light chaos*
◆ *dark order*
◆ *dark chaos*

Fire Elementals must be summoned directly into combat by an Overlord, Juggernaut Adept, or other Light Chaos spell-casting creature. As soon as the fight ends, the Fire Elemental disappears, whether or not it won the fight. Although Fire Elementals are single-use creatures, they are worth their casting cost–they hold Warrior rank, but they're more powerful than any other Light Chaos Warrior.

Tip

Fire Elementals can chain together melee attacks into combos with ease, but they're also capable of fighting an opponent from a distance with their impressive ranged attacks. Repeated use of the Fire Rift attack at the start of a fight sends your foe down in flames.

Rank: Warrior
Health Energy: 2
Magic Energy: 2
Movement Range:
Summon Only

Movement Type:
Summon Only
Army Builder Cost: n/a
Team Fighter Cost: 3
Resurrect Cost: 2.5
(Summon Elemental Spell)

FIRE ELEMENTAL MOVE LIST

Attack	Name
Light Melee	Quick Jab
Heavy Melee	Ranged Strike
Light Magic	Fire Rift
Heavy Magic	Fire Blast
Special Magic	Dive
Signature Attack	Impact Wave (LLLH)

Fire Rift

Impact Wave (Part 1)

Fire Blast

Impact Wave (Part 2)

Dive

Impact Wave (Part 3)

JUGGERNAUT ADEPT

Juggernaut Adepts are the only Light Chaos creatures other than Overlords that can cast spells on the World Map without having to use a Magic Amplifier. They're also fierce arena combat fighters, capable of unleashing punishing melee attacks as well as effective ranged attacks (Fireball, Grab & Throw). Remember that if you want to use the Grab & Throw spell, you need to be near a boulder that the Juggernaut Adept can magically raise into the air and hurl at an enemy.

Tip
The Juggernaut Adept's only weakness is its limited mobility. It's a slow and sluggish fighter; if you can keep hitting it and dodging its counterattacks, you can wear it down. But like a good heavyweight boxer, the Juggernaut Adept only needs to connect a few times to knock you out, so don't push your luck!

Rank: Champion
Health Energy: 3
Magic Energy: 2
Movement Range: 5 tiles

Movement Type: Walker
Army Builder Cost: 6
Team Fighter Cost: 4
Resurrect Cost: 4.5

JUGGERNAUT ADEPT MOVE LIST

Attack	Name
Light Melee	Head Jab
Heavy Melee	Spinning Head Thrust
Light Magic	Fireball
Heavy Magic	Grab & Throw
Special Magic	Ram Attack
Signature Attack	Magic Wave Attack (LLLH)

Fireball

Magic Wave Attack (Part 1)

Grab & Throw

Magic Wave Attack (Part 2)

Ram Attack

Magic Wave Attack (Part 3)

PRIMA'S OFFICIAL STRATEGY GUIDE

BLAZE DRAGON

Not only is the Blaze Dragon one of the largest Light Chaos creatures, it's also one of the fastest. Blaze Dragons can chain together combinations of melee attacks that slice a careless foe into strips within seconds, and their Dive ability lets them get out of any corner that an opponent back them into.

wrath unleashed chapter 3

overlords & creatures
- *light order*
- *light chaos*
- *dark order*
- *dark chaos*

Tip

A Blaze Dragon's size can work against it in combat, if you know how to exploit the weakness. Try to stun the Blaze Dragon and get around behind it, where the Blaze Dragon can't get to you without breaking away from combat. Its Breath attack is powerful, but it's also easy to predict and dodge.

Fireball

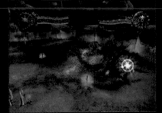

Scorpion Stinger (Part 1)

Rank: Champion
Health Energy: 3
Magic Energy: 2
Movement Range: 5 tiles

Movement Type: Flyer
Army Builder Cost: 5
Team Fighter Cost: 4
Resurrect Cost: 4.5

Breath

Scorpion Stinger (Part 2)

BLAZE DRAGON MOVE LIST

Attack	Name
Light Melee	Claw Swipe
Heavy Melee	Claw Thrust
Light Magic	Fireball
Heavy Magic	Breath
Special Magic	Dive
Signature Attack	Scorpion Stinger (LLLH while running)

Dive

Scorpion Stinger (Part 3)

OVERLORDS & CREATURES

FIRE GIANT

Fire Giants are the heavy hitters of the Light Chaos Champion ranks. While not as fast as Blaze Dragons or as powerful as Juggernaut Adepts, they are well-balanced fighters that can hold their own with fast and tough creatures alike. They're the ideal creatures in just about any combat situation, and their generous movement range lets them cross nearly any World Map in no time.

Tip
Not only does the Fire Giant's Cannonball attack do a great deal of damage, it also knocks the enemy back. This sets them up nicely for a few Fireballs, or even better, some enemy-seeking Summon attacks!

Rank: Champion
Health Energy: 3
Magic Energy: 2
Movement Range: 5 tiles

Movement Type: Walker
Army Builder Cost: 4
Team Fighter Cost: 4
Resurrect Cost: 4.5

FIRE GIANT MOVE LIST

Attack	Name
Light Melee	Single-Arm Strike
Heavy Melee	Double-Arm Swipe
Light Magic	Fireball
Heavy Magic	FireBlast
Special Magic	Summon
Signature Attack	Cannonball (LLLH)

Fireball

Cannonball (Part 1)

Fire Blast

Cannonball (Part 2)

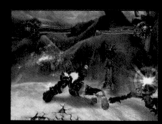
Summon

Cannonball (Part 3)

DEMIGOD

*wrath
unleashed
chapter 3*

*overlords
& creatures*

◆ *light order*
◆ *light chaos*
◆ *dark order*
◆ *dark chaos*

Epothos, the Light Order Demigod, fights with a fierceness that matches the fiery realm he rules. Every one of his melee attacks is accompanied with a blast of fire, and the attacks can be chained together into combos with great speed and ease. His Pole Vault Smash crushes any enemy unfortunate enough to be caught by it, and sends them flying halfway across the arena.

Tip

Epothos has several effective long-range attacks. His Fire Rift magic attack is good for softening up an enemy at the start of a fight. His Summon attack is a more powerful version of Fire Rift that chases enemies around the arena. Even his Fire Blast has a long reach and inflicts massive damage.

Fire Rift

Pole Vault Smash (Part 1)

Rank: Overlord	Movement Type: Walker
Health Energy: 5	Army Builder Cost: 8
Magic Energy: 3	Team Fighter Cost: 8
Movement Range: 5 tiles	Resurrect Cost: n/a

DEMIGOD MOVE LIST

Attack	Name
Light Melee	Light Fire Bolt
Heavy Melee	Heavy Fire Bolt
Light Magic	Fire Rift
Heavy Magic	Fire Blast
Special Magic	Summon
Signature Attack	Pole Vault Smash (LLLH while running)

Fire Blast

Pole Vault Smash (Part 2)

Summon

Pole Vault Smash (Part 3)

OVERLORDS & CREATURES

GOD

If you thought the Demigod form of Epothos was impressive, you'll be blown away by his God form! His new signature attack, Fire Storm Whirlwind, sends enemies shooting across the arena, badly wounded and on fire. His melee attacks are fast and deadly, and with an extra health orb, God Epothos is almost impossible to defeat in combat.

Tip

One of Epothos' newest and most deadly attacks is his Magma Inferno heavy magic spell. It takes a couple of seconds to cast, and Epothos is vulnerable when casting it, but a successful Magma Inferno takes out nearly a full orb of health from his adversary. The only defense against it is a Magic Shield or a successful attack on Epothos while he's casting it. Cast it from a distance to prevent your enemy from interrupting it.

Rank: Overlord
Health Energy: 5
Magic Energy: 3
Movement Range: 5 tiles

Movement Type: Flyer
Army Builder Cost: 12
Team Fighter Cost: 10
Resurrect Cost: n/a

GOD MOVE LIST

Attack	Name
Light Melee	Light Fire Bolt
Heavy Melee	Heavy Fire Bolt
Light Magic	Fire Rift
Heavy Magic	Magma Inferno
Special Magic	Summon
Signature Attack	Fire Storm Whirlwind (LLLH while running)

Fire Rift

Fire Storm Whirlwind (Part 1)

Magma Inferno

Fire Storm Whirlwind (Part 2)

Summon

Fire Storm Whirlwind (Part 3)

WRATH UNLEASHED
UNLEASHED
PRIMA'S OFFICIAL STRATEGY GUIDE

DARK ⊙ ORDER

*wrath
unleashed
chapter 3*

*overlords
& creatures*

◆ *light order*
◆ *light chaos*
◆ *dark order*
◆ *dark chaos*

DARK ORDER CREATURES AT A GLANCE

Name	Rank	Health Orbs*	Magic Orbs*	Movement Range	Movement Type**	Army Builder Cost	Team Fighter Cost	Resurrect Cost***
Centabra	Sentinel	1	1	3	Walker	1	1	1.5
Dark Unicorn	Sentinel	1	1	2	Teleporter	1	1	1.5
Spirit Armor	Warrior	2	1	4	Walker	2	2	3
Djinn	Warrior	2	1	3	Flyer	2	2	
Earth Elemental	Warrior	2	2	Summon Only	Summon Only	n/a	3	2.5 (Summon)
Nightmare Adept	Champion	3	2	5	Walker	6	4	4.5
Arch Demon	Champion	3	2	5	Flyer	5	4	4.5
Iron Golem	Champion	3	2	5	Walker	4	4	4.5
Demigod	Overlord	4	3	5	Walker	8	8	n/a
God	Overlord	5	3	5	Flyer	12	10	n/a

* *Health orbs* and *magic orbs* in the table also include the full bar of health or magic energy the creature starts out with.

** *Movement type* indicates what terrain the creature can cross. *Teleporters* can cross gaps and tiles occupied by other creatures. *Flyers* can cross tiles occupied by other creatures but cannot cross gaps. *Walkers* can't cross gaps or tiles occupied by other creatures.

*** *Resurrect cost* is the number of Mana orbs required to resurrect the creature.

OVERLORDS & CREATURES

CENTABRA

Centabras are the grunts of the Dark Order army. They're excellent for seizing unoccupied Mana Wats and Temples, and they're handy in arena combat, despite being among the weakest creatures in the game. Centabras are quick enough to hit their foes and back off quickly, allowing them to face off against foes with much more health energy.

Tip

When using a Centabra in combat, lead off with several Throw Weapon attacks to soften up your foe.

Rank: Sentinel	Movement Type: Walker
Health Energy: 1	Army Builder Cost: 1
Magic Energy: 1	Team Fighter Cost: 1
Movement Range: 3 tiles	Resurrect Cost: 2

CENTABRA MOVE LIST

Attack	Name
Light Melee	Quick Axe Slash
Heavy Melee	Heavy Axe Slash
Light Magic	Throw Weapon
Heavy Magic	Trap
Special Magic	Ram Attack
Signature Attack	Back Kick (LLLH while running)

Note

Centabras, like all Sentinels, have the Sentinel Barrier ability, which means they can't be attacked by creatures unless those creatures began their turns on a tile adjacent to the Centabra. Also, creatures can't move past Centabras unless they defeat the Centabras in combat.

Throw Weapon

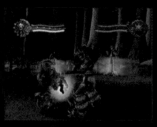
Back Kick (Part 1)

Trap

Back Kick (Part 2)

Ram Attack

Back Kick (Part 3)

PRIMA'S OFFICIAL STRATEGY GUIDE

DARK UNICORN

overlords
& creatures
◆ light order
◆ light chaos
◆ dark order
◆ dark chaos

Like Centabras, Dark Unicorns are Sentinels, but where Centabras are more effective in arena combat, Dark Unicorns shine on the World Map. Although they are among the weakest creatures in the game, they are also the only teleporting creatures in the Dark Order army, which allows them to cross gaps on the World Map to occupy Temples or to position themselves to act as blockers with their Sentinel Barrier power.

Tip
Dark Unicorns don't have the health or power to get into arena fights, so execute hit-and-run attacks in arena combat. Use Throw Weapon to draw first blood, and use Blink if your enemy gets too close for comfort. Finally, if you have to get into melee combat, try to pull off an Energy Bolt, which does a great deal of damage and sends your opponent flying.

Rank: Sentinel
Health Energy: 1
Magic Energy: 1
Movement Range: 2 tiles
Movement Type: Teleporter
Army Builder Cost: 1
Team Fighter Cost: 1
Resurrect Cost: 2

DARK UNICORN MOVE LIST

Attack	Name
Light Melee	Horn Jab
Heavy Melee	Horn Slice
Light Magic	Throw Weapon
Heavy Magic	Lightning Blast
Special Magic	Blink
Signature Attack	Energy Bolt (LLLH while running)

Note
Dark Unicorns, like all Sentinels, have the Sentinel Barrier ability, which means they can't be attacked by creatures unless those creatures began their turns on a tile adjacent to the Dark Unicorns. Also, creatures can't move past Dark Unicorns unless they defeat the Dark Unicorns in combat.

Throw Weapon

Energy Bolt (Part 1)

Lightning Blast

Energy Bolt (Part 2)

Blink

Energy Bolt (Part 3)

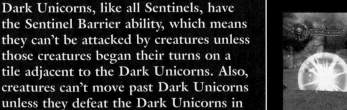

SPIRIT ARMOR

These ethereal Warriors strike terror into the hearts of their adversaries with their otherworldly auras and their formidable battle prowess. Armed with a staff and a shield that it uses in melee attacks, a Spirit Armor is an excellent, low-cost creature to send against weaker enemies. The creature's Whirling Uppercut signature attack does a tremendous amount of damage and sends its victim flying across the arena.

Tip

While Spirit Armors are better at melee combat than magical duels, their Throw Weapon spell is a great way to get a few free hits in on an enemy at the start of combat, and, at close ranges, the Shield Blast also sends your foes reeling.

Rank: Warrior	Movement Type: Walker
Health Energy: 2	Army Builder Cost: 2
Magic Energy: 1	Team Fighter Cost: 2
Movement Range: 4 tiles	Resurrect Cost: 3

SPIRIT ARMOR MOVE LIST

Attack	Name
Light Melee	Shield Strike
Heavy Melee	Staff Strike
Light Magic	Throw Weapon
Heavy Magic	Shield Blast
Special Magic	Magic Shield
Signature Attack	Whirling Uppercut (LLLH)

Throw Weapon

Whirling Uppercut (Part 1)

Shield Blast

Whirling Uppercut (Part 2)

Magic Shield

Whirling Uppercut (Part 3)

DJINN

Djinns are fast, deadly spirits that can link melee attacks into vicious combos with the greatest of ease. They dodge and strafe quickly, and their Blink ability lets them instantly teleport around the combat arena and out of danger. Their Steal Life ability is slow to use, but it not only reduces your foe's health, it also replenishes some of the Djinn's!

Tip

The best way to take on a Djinn is to hit first and stay on top of them. If you have attacks that can freeze or stun the Djinn, use them liberally.

Ground Wake

Whirling Blade (Part 1)

Steal Life

Whirling Blade (Part 2)

Blink

Whirling Blade (Part 3)

wrath unleashed chapter 3

overlords & creatures
- *light order*
- *light chaos*
- *dark order*
- *dark chaos*

Rank: Warrior	Movement Type: Flyer
Health Energy: 2	Army Builder Cost: 2
Magic Energy: 1	Team Fighter Cost: 2
Movement Range: 3 tiles	Resurrect Cost: 3

DJINN MOVE LIST

Attack	Name
Light Melee	Staff Jab
Heavy Melee	Staff Thrust
Light Magic	Ground Wake
Heavy Magic	Steal Life
Special Magic	Blink
Signature Attack	Whirling Blade (LLHH while running)

EARTH ELEMENTAL

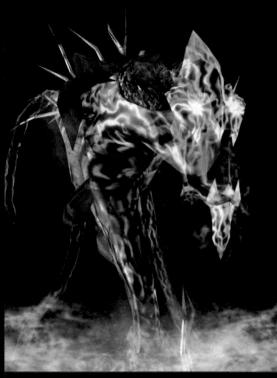

Earth Elementals can be summoned into combat by Overlords and Adepts for a single fight. They must be summoned directly into combat with an enemy creature, and the Earth Elemental disappears after the fight, regardless of who won. Earth Elementals are the most powerful Warrior creatures in the Dark Order; their prowess in battle more than compensates for their high cost and single-use status.

Tip

While Earth Elemental magic is formidable in arena combat, it's the melee attack that really makes the creature such an excellent Warrior. Earth Elementals can chain together combos without much effort, and no other Dark Order Warrior has such a potent combination of range and power in its melee attack.

Rank: Warrior
Health Energy: 2
Magic Energy: 2
Movement Range:
Summon Only

Movement Type:
Summon Only
Army Builder Cost: n/a
Team Fighter Cost: 3
Resurrect Cost: 2.5

EARTH ELEMENTAL MOVE LIST

Attack	Name
Light Melee	Quick Jab
Heavy Melee	Ranged Strike
Light Magic	Ground Quake
Heavy Magic	Earth Blast
Special Magic	Dive
Signature Attack	Elemental Twister (LLHH while running)

Ground Quake

Elemental Twister (Part 1)

Earth Blast

Elemental Twister (Part 2)

Dive

Elemental Twister (Part 3)

NIGHTMARE ADEPT

wrath unleashed chapter 3

overlords & creatures
- *light order*
- *light chaos*
- *dark order*
- *dark chaos*

These horrific beasts are the Adept Champions of the Dark Order army on the World Map or in a Battle arena. As spell casters with a generous movement range, they can be used for a variety of tasks on the World Map, from teleporting troops into combat to occupying distant Temples. Their large reserves of health energy allow them to administer ruthless beat-downs, and their Steal Life magic ensures that they can keep themselves in fighting shape while draining their opponents dry.

Tip

The only real weakness of a Nightmare Adept is its lack of speed. A quick adversary can get several hits in on a Nightmare Adept. And while its Summon and Ground Wake spells are tough to counter in arena combat, it is also vulnerable to ranged attacks. It takes a Nightmare Adept a while to close the distance between itself and its adversary.

Rank: Champion	Movement Type: Walker
Health Energy: 3	Army Builder Cost: 6
Magic Energy: 2	Team Fighter Cost: 4
Movement Range: 5 tiles	Resurrect Cost: 4.5

NIGHTMARE ADEPT MOVE LIST

Attack	Name
Light Melee	Tentacle Slap
Heavy Melee	Light Sword Strike
Light Magic	Ground Wake
Heavy Magic	Steal Life
Special Magic	Summon
Signature Attack	Adept Energy Slash (LLHH while running)

Ground Wake

Adept Energy Slash (Part 1)

Steal Life

Adept Energy Slash (Part 2)

Summon

Adept Energy Slash (Part 3)

OVERLORDS & CREATURES

ARCH DEMON

Arch Demons are the elite troops of the Dark Order army, and they are horrifying adversaries for any creature. Although a bit slow, Arch Demons can execute withering combinations of melee attacks, using their hands, feet, and even wings as weapons. They're also no slouches in the magic department, with formidable short-range (Earth Blast) and long-range (Ground Wake) attacks.

Tip
You can use the Jump Stun ability to land near your opponent and damage and stun it simultaneously. It's also a handy move to use when you're backed into a corner–it lets you fly right over your foe's head!

Rank: Champion	Movement Type: Flyer
Health Energy: 3	Army Builder Cost: 5
Magic Energy: 2	Team Fighter Cost: 4
Movement Range: 5 tiles	Resurrect Cost: 4.5

ARCH DEMON MOVE LIST

Attack	Name
Light Melee	Claw Slash
Heavy Melee	Kick Slash
Light Magic	Ground Wake
Heavy Magic	Earth Blast
Special Magic	Jump Stun
Signature Attack	Dual Wing Slam (LLLH)

Ground Wake

Dual Wing Slam (Part 1)

Earth Blast

Dual Wing Slam (Part 2)

Jump Stun

Dual Wing Slam (Part 3)

IRON GOLEM

Iron Golems add new meaning to the term "heavy metal." These clanking monstrosities are little more than animated piles of scrap metal, held together by a magnetic core. They are fearsome in melee combat, with ranged melee attacks that inflict serious damage. Their magic attacks aren't to be underestimated either. One of the Iron Golem's most unique and devastating attacks is the Gravity Well, which pulls an adversary toward the Iron Golem's whirling fists.

Tip
Backed into a corner? Execute a Flying Iron Crash, which not only knocks your foe's health meter down a few pegs but also gets the Iron Golem well clear of its adversary.

Rank: Champion	Movement Type: Walker
Health Energy: 3	Army Builder Cost: 4
Magic Energy: 2	Team Fighter Cost: 4
Movement Range: 5 tiles	Resurrect Cost: 4.5

IRON GOLEM MOVE LIST

Attack	Name
Light Melee	Single Punch
Heavy Melee	Double Punch
Light Magic	Ground Wake
Heavy Magic	Shield Blast
Special Magic	Gravity Well
Signature Attack	Flying Iron Crash (LLLH while running)

Ground Wake

Flying Iron Crash (Part 1)

Shield Blast

Flying Iron Crash (Part 2)

Gravity Well

Flying Iron Crash (Part 3)

DEMIGOD

Durlock has a reputation for being a cold fish, aloof and distant from his fellow Overlords. But in combat, Durlock has a fiery passion that rivals that of Epothos. Like all Overlords, Durlock is fast and chains together melee combos effortlessly. His signature attack, Staff Slam Spikes, takes out nearly a full bar's worth of health and sends his enemy stumbling backwards–a perfect target for Durlock's formidable ranged attacks, Ground Quake and Summon.

Tip

One of Durlock's greatest assets is his tremendous speed. Even if wounded, Durlock can usually stay out of the reach of his opponent. Thanks to his tremendous magic energy reserves, he can pepper his foe with melee attacks from a safe distance if he has to.

Rank: Overlord	Movement Type: Walker
Health Energy: 4	Army Builder Cost: 8
Magic Energy: 3	Team Fighter Cost: 8
Movement Range: 5 tiles	Resurrect Cost: n/a

DEMIGOD MOVE LIST

Attack	Name
Light Melee	Light Bolt
Heavy Melee	Ground Strike
Light Magic	Ground Quake
Heavy Magic	Earth Blast
Special Magic	Summon
Signature Attack	Staff Slam Spikes (LLLH)

Ground Quake

Staff Slam Spikes (Part 1)

Earth Blast

Staff Slam Spikes (Part 2)

Summon

Staff Slam Spikes (Part 3)

GOD

*wrath
unleashed
chapter 3*

*overlords
& creatures*

◆ *light order*
◆ *light chaos*
◆ *dark order*
◆ *dark chaos*

As a Demigod, Durlock is a formidable foe. As a God, he is almost invincible. All his attacks are slightly faster and more powerful in God mode than in Demigod mode. His combos are even more crushing, and his Earth Wall Summon signature attack is an even more brutal version of Staff Slam Spikes.

Tip

Durlock's most powerful spell is Gaia's Rage, which can be cast from anywhere in the arena and hits his adversary without fail for nearly a full health bar's worth of damage. The only defense against it is a Magic Shield or a successful attack on Durlock while he's casting the spell.

Ground Quake

Earth Wall Summon (Part 1)

Rank: Overlord	Movement Type: Flyer
Health Energy: 5	Army Builder Cost: 12
Magic Energy: 3	Team Fighter Cost: 10
Movement Range: 5 tiles	Resurrect Cost: n/a

GOD MOVE LIST

Attack	Name
Light Melee	Light Bolt
Heavy Melee	Magic Lance
Light Magic	Ground Quake
Heavy Magic	Gaia's Rage
Special Magic	Summon
Signature Attack	Earth Wall Summon (LLLH)

Gaia's Rage

Earth Wall Summon (Part 2)

Summon

Earth Wall Summon (Part 3)

DARK CHAOS

DARK CHAOS CREATURES AT A GLANCE

Name	Rank	Health Orbs*	Magic Orbs*	Movement Range	Movement Type**	Army Builder Cost	Team Fighter Cost	Resurrect Cost***
Centa	Sentinel	1	1	3	Walker	1	1	1.5
Dark Unicorn	Sentinel	1	1	2	Teleporter	1	1	1.5
Spirit Armor	Warrior	2	1	4	Walker	2	2	3
Djinn	Warrior	2	1	3	Flyer	2	2	3
Wind Elemental	Warrior	2	2	Summon Only	Summon Only	n/a	3	2.5 (Summon)
Nightmare Adept	Champion	3	2	5	Walker	6	4	4.5
Chaos Demon	Champion	3	2	5	Flyer	5	4	4.5
Cyc	Champion	3	2	5	Walker	4	4	4.5
Demigod	Overlord	4	3	5	Walker	8	8	n/a
God	Overlord	5	3	5	Flyer	12	10	n/a

* *Health orbs* and *magic orbs* in the table also include the full bar of health or magic energy the creature starts out with.

** *Movement type* indicates what terrain the creature can cross. *Teleporters* can cross gaps and tiles occupied by other creatures. *Flyers* can cross tiles occupied by other creatures but cannot cross gaps. *Walkers* can't cross gaps or tiles occupied by other creatures.

*** *Resurrect cost* is the number of Mana orbs required to resurrect the creature.

CENTABRA

Use Centabras to conquer and hold unoccupied structures, such as Temples and Mana Wats. Their Sentinel Barrier ability ensures that distant enemies won't be able to attack them for at least two turns. And even though they're on the low end of the Dark Chaos power scale, Centabras usually hold their own in combat quite well, with a variety of quick attacks and combos that can send even the toughest foes reeling.

Tip

Start out fights with a generous helping of Throw Weapon spells. These soften up opponents quickly before the fight begins in earnest. Follow up with quick attacks and combos, and be sure to use the Centabra's speed to dodge the counterattacks.

Rank: Sentinel	Movement Type: Walker
Health Energy: 1	Army Builder Cost: 1
Magic Energy: 1	Team Fighter Cost: 1
Movement Range: 3 tiles	Resurrect Cost: 2

CENTABRA MOVE LIST

Attack	Name
Light Melee	Light Axe Slash
Heavy Melee	Heavy Axe Slash
Light Magic	Throw Weapon
Heavy Magic	Trap
Special Magic	Ram Attack
Signature Attack	Back Kick (LLHH while running)

Note

Centabras, like all Sentinels, have the Sentinel Barrier ability, which means they can't be attacked by creatures unless those creatures began their turns on a tile adjacent to the Centabra. Also, creatures can't move past Centabras unless they defeat the Centabras in combat.

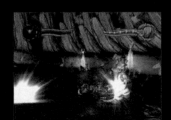

Throw Weapon

Back Kick (Part 1)

Trap

Back Kick (Part 2)

Ram Attack

Back Kick (Part 3)

DARK UNICORN

Dark Unicorns are Sentinels that rely upon their natural speed and maneuverability to survive. Arguably the weakest creatures in the Dark Chaos army, Dark Unicorns are the only creatures that can naturally teleport on the World Map, allowing them to cross gaps and reach areas that other creatures can't. In combat, Dark Unicorns suffer from a lack of power and health reserves, but they're skilled at staying out of harm's way, thanks to their innate speed and Blink ability.

Tip
Dark Unicorns don't have the strength or stamina to get into a slugfest with rival creatures. Use hit-and-run techniques, such as the Energy Bolt signature attack, to inflict damage and open distance between you and your opponent.

Rank: Sentinel	Movement Type: Teleporter
Health Energy: 1	Army Builder Cost: 1
Magic Energy: 1	Team Fighter Cost: 1
Movement Range: 2 tiles	Resurrect Cost: 2

DARK UNICORN MOVE LIST

Attack	Name
Light Melee	Horn Jab
Heavy Melee	Horn Slice
Light Magic	Throw Weapon
Heavy Magic	Lightning Blast
Special Magic	Blink
Signature Attack	Energy Bolt (LLLH while running)

Note
Dark Unicorns, like all Sentinels, have the Sentinel Barrier ability, which means they can't be attacked by creatures unless those creatures began their turns on a tile adjacent to the Dark Unicorns. Also, creatures can't move past Dark Unicorns unless they defeat the Dark Unicorns in combat.

Throw Weapon

Energy Bolt (Part 1)

Lightning Blast

Energy Bolt (Part 2)

Blink

Energy Bolt (Part 3)

SPIRIT ARMOR

*wrath
unleashed
chapter 3*

*overlords
& creatures*
◆ *light order*
◆ *light chaos*
◆ *dark order*
◆ *dark chaos*

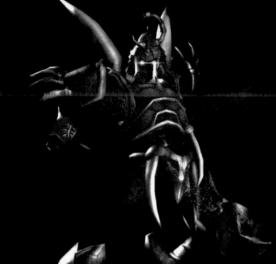

These spectral axemen might appear intangible, but their axe and shield never fail to make a very physical impression on their adversaries. Stronger than Djinns, Spirit Armors are the "shock troops" of the Dark Chaos army, best used to challenge smaller, weaker creatures that have occupied Temples or other structures of strategic importance.

Tip
Open combat with a few Throw Weapon spells, and quickly close the distance between you and your foe so you can take advantage of the Spirit Armor's ruthless melee attack combos.

Rank: Warrior	Movement Type: Walker
Health Energy: 2	Army Builder Cost: 2
Magic Energy: 1	Team Fighter Cost: 2
Movement Range: 4 tiles	Resurrect Cost: 3

SPIRIT ARMOR MOVE LIST

Attack	Name
Light Melee	Shield Strike
Heavy Melee	Staff Strike
Light Magic	Throw Weapon
Heavy Magic	Shield Blast
Special Magic	Magic Shield
Signature Attack	Energy Expand Blast (LLLH while running)

Throw Weapon

Energy Expand Blast (Part 1)

Shield Blast

Energy Expand Blast (Part 2)

Magic Shield

Energy Expand Blast (Part 3)

DJINN

These mischievous spirits are accomplished in the arts of magic and melee combat, and their flying ability lets them cover a lot of ground on the World Map as well. Djinns are well known for their crushing attack combos, executed with lightning speed and ferocity. They can also escape from any sticky situation with their Blink ability, provided that they have the magic energy to use it.

Tip

The Djinn's light magic attack, Ball Lightning, moves more slowly than the light magic attacks of other realm's Warriors. However, the Ball Lightning also sends out arcs of electricity to zap any creature who gets close to the attack, so you don't have to be as accurate with Ball Lightning as you might with other creatures' light magic attacks.

Rank: Warrior
Health Energy: 2
Magic Energy: 1
Movement Range: 3 tiles

Movement Type: Flyer
Army Builder Cost: 2
Team Fighter Cost: 2
Resurrect Cost: 3

DJINN MOVE LIST

Attack	Name
Light Melee	Staff Jab
Heavy Melee	Staff Thrust
Light Magic	Ball Lightning
Heavy Magic	Trap
Special Magic	Blink
Signature Attack	1,000 Whirlwinds (LLLH)

Ball Lightning

1,000 Whirlwinds (Part 1)

Trap

1,000 Whirlwinds (Part 2)

Blink

1,000 Whirlwinds (Part 3)

WIND ELEMENTAL

Like other realms' Elementals, Wind Elementals are summoned into combat by a spell-casting creature and only stick around for one fight, regardless of whether or not the Wind Elemental wins it. Wind Elementals justify their casting cost and short life span with their speed and power. They are easily the most powerful and effective Dark Chaos Warriors when it comes to arena combat.

Tip

If you use the Wind Elementals' Dive spell, it sinks into the ground and moves under the surface. It is immune to all attacks as long as it's submerged. Release the Special Magic button and the Wind Elemental pops out of the ground. If you appear underneath your opponent, you deal out some serious damage.

Rank: Warrior	Movement Type:
Health Energy: 2	Summon Only
Magic Energy: 2	Army Builder Cost: n/a
Movement Range:	Team Fighter Cost: 3
Summon Only	Resurrect Cost: 2.5
	(Summon Elemental Spell)

WIND ELEMENTAL MOVE LIST

Attack	Name
Light Melee	Quick Jab
Heavy Melee	Ranged Strike
Light Magic	Lightning Arc
Heavy Magic	Lightning Blast
Special Magic	Dive
Signature Attack	Elemental Twister (LLHH while running)

Lightning Arc

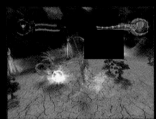
Elemental Twister (Part 1)

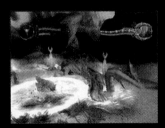
Lightning Blast

Elemental Twister (Part 2)

Dive

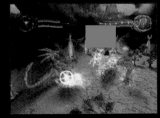
Elemental Twister (Part 3)

NIGHTMARE ADEPT

Nightmare Adepts wield magic in arena combat and on the World Map to augment their already impressive physical skills. On the World Map, Nightmare Adepts can cast any spell except Resurrect and Wrath, allowing a player to use World Map spells without putting their Overlord at risk. Their Ball Lightning and Grab & Throw spells allow them to decimate foes from a distance, and their melee combat skills aren't too shabby either.

Tip

A Nightmare Adept's biggest weakness is its slow movement and attack speed. An adversary who specializes in quick attacks and dodges can hit the Nightmare Adept repeatedly and avoid counterattacks. The best way to deal with a Nightmare Adept is from a distance, or with a creature capable of executing fast combo attacks that can keep it off balance.

Rank: Champion
Health Energy: 3
Magic Energy: 2
Movement Range: 5 tiles

Movement Type: Walker
Army Builder Cost: 6
Team Fighter Cost: 4
Resurrect Cost: 4.5

NIGHTMARE ADEPT MOVE LIST

Attack	Name
Light Melee	Tentacle Slap
Heavy Melee	Light Sword Strike
Light Magic	Ball Lightning
Heavy Magic	Grab & Throw
Special Magic	Blink
Signature Attack	Whirlwind Hooves (LLLH)

Ball Lightning

Whirlwind Hooves (Part 1)

Grab & Throw

Whirlwind Hooves (Part 2)

Blink

Whirlwind Hooves (Part 3)

CHAOS DEMON

*wrath
unleashed
chapter 3*

*overlords
& creatures*
◆ *light order*
◆ *light chaos*
◆ *dark order*
◆ *dark chaos*

These gargoyle-like creatures are among the Dark Chaos army's hardiest Champions. Gifted with the ability to fly, they can cover a great deal of ground on the World Map, and they can also leap over enemies and stun them in arena combat with their Jump Stun ability. They have an impressive array of melee attacks, and while their combos might be slower to execute than other creatures', the power behind them is all but unmatched.

Tip

Don't forget the Chaos Demon's ranged attacks. Ball Lightning is a slow and weak attack, but it's accurate and hard to dodge. Lightning Gaze, on the other hand, can hit an opponent on the other side of the arena and send it flying.

Rank: Champion	Movement Type: Flyer
Health Energy: 3	Army Builder Cost: 5
Magic Energy: 2	Team Fighter Cost: 4
Movement Range: 5 tiles	Resurrect Cost: 4.5

CHAOS DEMON MOVE LIST

Attack	Name
Light Melee	Claw Swipe
Heavy Melee	Claw Thrust
Light Magic	Ball Lightning
Heavy Magic	Lighting Gaze
Special Magic	Jump Stun
Signature Attack	Double Energy Blast (LLHH)

Ball Lightning

Double Energy Blast (Part 1)

Lightning Gaze

Double Energy Blast (Part 2)

Jump Stun

Double Energy Blast (Part 3)

CYCLOPS

Cyclopes are huge, aggressive beasts with combat speed that belies their bulk. Their combos are a furious flurry of claws and kicks that whittle just about any adversary down to size in no time. When used in conjunction with the Stun Smash, which temporarily immobilizes an enemy, their melee attacks are almost unequaled in destructive power.

Tip
Almost all Cyclops attacks are close-range attacks. If you can keep your distance and use ranged attacks, you can avoid most of its deadliest moves.

Ball Lighting

Rolling Claw Smash (Part 1)

Stun Smash

Rolling Claw Smash (Part 2)

Ram Attack

Rolling Claw Smash (Part 3)

Rank: Champion
Health Energy: 3
Magic Energy: 2
Movement Range: 5 tiles

Movement Type: Walker
Army Builder Cost: 4
Team Fighter Cost: 4
Resurrect Cost: 4.5

CYCLOPS MOVE LIST

Attack	Name
Light Melee	Claw Jab
Heavy Melee	Claw Thrust
Light Magic	Ball Lightning
Heavy Magic	Stun Smash
Special Magic	Ram Attack
Signature Attack	Rolling Claw Smash (LLLH while running)

DEMIGOD

Off the battlefield, Helamis is a crafty schemer who will stop at nothing to call Epothos and the Throne of Gaia hers. In arena combat, she strings together chains of devastating combos that inflict traumatic amounts of damage in the blink of an eye. Her melee attacks aren't as powerful as those of some of the other Overlords, but her speed is unmatched among the rulers of the Shattered Realms.

Tip

Use speed to your advantage in combat. Flip Kicks bring Helamis in close to her enemy and provide the first hit of a combo at the same time. Her Lightning Gaze can keep foes at a distance while inflicting severe damage on them.

wrath unleashed chapter 3

overlords & creatures
- *light order*
- *light chaos*
- *dark order*
- *dark chaos*

Fire Rift

Kiss of Death (Part 1)

Rank: Overlord	Movement Type: Walker
Health Energy: 4	Army Builder Cost: 8
Magic Energy: 3	Team Fighter Cost: 8
Movement Range: 5 tiles	Resurrect Cost: n/a

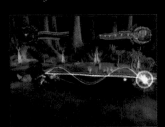

Fire Blast

Kiss of Death (Part 2)

DEMIGOD MOVE LIST

Attack	Name
Light Melee	Staff Slash
Heavy Melee	Flip Kick
Light Magic	Lightning Arc
Heavy Magic	Lightning Gaze
Special Magic	Blink
Signature Attack	Kiss of Death (LLLH while running)

Summon

Kiss of Death (Part 3)

OVERLORDS & CREATURES

GOD

In her God form, Helamis is practically invincible, which is good news for Dark Chaos and bad news for all three other realms. Her already unmatched speed is increased even more, and all her attacks and combos inflict slightly more damage. She also learns the Staff Seduction Blast, which is even more powerful than the Kiss of Death.

Tip

Use the Sky's Embrace heavy magic attack from a distance. If cast properly (which takes a couple of seconds), it inflicts tremendous damage. But Helamis is completely vulnerable when casting it, and if she's attacked, the spell is disrupted. You can cast Sky's Embrace anywhere in the Battle arena. It hits your foe no matter how they try to dodge, provided that the spell is not interrupted.

Rank: Overlord
Health Energy: 5
Magic Energy: 3
Movement Range: 5 tiles

Movement Type: Flyer
Army Builder Cost: 12
Team Fighter Cost: 10
Resurrect Cost: n/a

GOD MOVE LIST

Attack	Name
Light Melee	Light Jab
Heavy Melee	Spin Kick
Light Magic	Lightning Arc
Heavy Magic	Sky's Embrace
Special Magic	Blink
Signature Attack	Staff Seduction Blast (LLLH while running)

Lightning Arc

Staff Seduction Blast (Part 1)

Sky's Embrace

Staff Seduction Blast (Part 2)

Blink

Staff Seduction Blast (Part 3)

MAGIC SPELLS

CASTING SPELLS

Choose the spell you want to cast from the Cast menu.

*wrath
unleashed
chapter 4*

magic spells
♦ *casting spells*
♦ *spells*

To cast spells in *Wrath Unleashed*, highlight a spell-casting creature and choose Cast from the small menu that appears when you select the creature. This brings up the Cast menu, a list of the eight spells that can be cast.

Note

Not all spells can be cast at all times. If you don't have enough Mana to cast a particular spell, or if the creature you have selected is not capable of casting that spell, the spell appears gray in the Cast menu.

Mana

The purple Mana bar and orbs in the upper-left corner of the screen represent your Mana.

At the beginning of each turn, your army regenerates some Mana (if you have creatures standing on a temple, citadel, or Mana-Wat), which is used to cast spells on the World Map. Your Mana is displayed as a purple bar and a row of purple orbs in the upper-left corner of the screen. One full purple bar is equivalent to half a purple Mana orb; each time the purple bar is completely filled with Mana, another half-orb appears under it.

Note

Your army's Mana, which is used to cast spells on the World Map, is not the same as your individual creatures' magic power, which is used to perform magical attacks in arena combat.

If your army has occupied any Citadels, Temples, or Mana Wats, you regenerate more Mana at the start of your turn. Citadels and Mana Wats provide twice as much Mana as Temples.

Tip

If you are playing on a World Map that requires you to capture a certain number of Temples for victory, send your creatures out to capture Temples rather than Mana Wats. This may put you at a slight disadvantage in terms of Mana regeneration, but you have to focus on the big picture, which is winning the war on the World Map.

Spell Casters

Only three types of creatures can cast spells in *Wrath Unleashed*: Demigod Overlords, God Overlords, and Adepts. Adepts cannot cast Wrath or Resurrect.

ADEPTS

Army	Adepts
Light Order	Juggernaut Adept
Light Chaos	Juggernaut Adept
Dark Order	Nightmare Adept
Dark Chaos	Nightmare Adept

MAGIC SPELLS

Immunity from Magic

Temples and Citadels confer magic immunity on the creatures that occupy them.

Creatures on Temples and Citadels are protected from magic of any type, friendly or hostile. Even if a Temple or Citadel is unoccupied, it is still magic-resistant (which means you can't cast Transform Land onto a tile that has a Temple or Citadel on it).

Keep in mind that, while magic resistance can be a huge asset to a creature, it can also be a drawback. For example, if a badly wounded creature is occupying a Temple, it will regenerate some health each turn thanks to the Temple's restorative properties. But that creature cannot have Heal or Transfer Health cast upon it, which could restore the creature's health much more quickly.

SPELLS

Eight spells can be cast in *Wrath Unleashed*. Knowing how and when to cast them can mean the difference between victory and defeat.

Bind

Cost: ○○○●●●
Casters: Adept, Overlord (Demigod and God)
Range: Target enemy creature must be within five tiles from caster.

How to Cast:
1. Select spell from Cast menu.
2. Select target enemy creature.

When Bind is cast on an enemy creature, that creature can't move off its tile or cast spells for three rounds. Bound creatures can still defend themselves in arena combat if attacked, however.

> ## Tip
> If an enemy Overlord or his Adepts are foolish enough to approach within five tiles of your Adepts or Overlord, Bind them quickly to prevent them from casting spells.

Heal

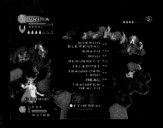

Resurrect

*wrath
unleashed
chapter 4*

magic spells
- *casting spells*
- *spells*

Cost: ◠◠◠◖●●

Casters: Adept, Overlord (Demigod and God)

Range: Target friendly creature must be within five tiles from caster.

How to Cast:
1. Select spell from Cast menu.
2. Select a friendly creature to heal.

Cast Heal on a friendly creature to fully replenish its health, regardless of how injured it is or what its maximum health capacity is.

Tip

You can't Heal severely injured units that have occupied Citadels or Temples, so you might want to consider keeping your wounded away from these structures until you can cast Heal on them.

Cost: Variable (see table below)

Casters: Overlord only (Demigod and God)

Range: Resurrected creature must appear on a tile adjacent to the caster.

How to Cast:
1. Select your Demigod or God.
2. Select spell from Cast menu.
3. Select creature from menu.
4. Select adjacent tile on which resurrected creature will appear.

Resurrect is an expensive spell, but it's one of the most powerful ones in your arsenal–so powerful, in fact, that only Overlords (Demigods and Gods) can cast it. Resurrect revives one of your fallen creatures on a tile adjacent to the caster. The more powerful the creature, the higher the casting cost.

Tip

You can only Resurrect your own creatures that have fallen in combat since the beginning of the current game. Save up your Mana so that you can Resurrect a powerful creature later in the game, rather than waste Mana on smaller creatures. It is best used to summon creatures to defend your Overlord.

MAGIC SPELLS

RESURRECT MANA COSTS BY CREATURE

Creature	Cost
Centaur/Centabra	◐○●●●●
Unicorn/Dark Unicorn	◐○●●●●
Giantess/Spirit Armor	◐○○●●●
Genie/Djinn	○○○●●●
Juggernaut/Nightmare (Adepts)	○○○○○◐
Frost Dragon/Blaze Dragon Arch Demon/Chaos Demon	○○○○○◐
Ogre Mage/Fire Giant Iron Golem/Cyclops	○○○○○◐

Summon Elemental

Cost: ○○◐●●●

Casters: Adept, Overlord (Demigod and God)

Range: Target enemy creature must be within three tiles of caster.

How to Cast:

1. Select spell from Cast menu.
2. Select target enemy creature for Elemental to attack.

When cast, this spell summons a powerful Elemental directly into combat with an enemy creature of your choice within three tiles of the caster. The Elemental dissipates at the end of one round, even if the Elemental won the arena battle against the enemy creature.

> ## Tip
> Summon Elemental is a great spell to use for a quick hit on a powerful enemy creature. Even if the Elemental loses the fight, it's practically guaranteed to take a toll on its adversary.

ELEMENTAL TYPES, BY CASTER

Caster Alignment	Elemental
Light Order	Water Elemental
Light Chaos	Fire Elemental
Dark Order	Earth Elemental
Dark Chaos	Wind Elemental

Teleport

Cost: ○○●●●●

Casters: Adept, Overlord (Demigod and God)

Range: Target must be within five tiles of caster and can teleport onto any other tile within five tiles of caster.

How to Cast:

1. Select spell from Cast menu.
2. Select creature to be Teleported (casters can Teleport themselves).
3. Select tile to Teleport creature to.

Teleport is an excellent way to bring creatures from the rear into the thick of battle in a hurry. Creatures within five tiles of the caster can be instantly transported onto any other tile within five tiles of the caster, which means that a creature could be sent as far as 11 tiles in a single round, if the caster is properly positioned. Casters can also Teleport themselves.

> # Tip
> Creatures can be Teleported directly into battle by sending them to a tile occupied by an enemy creature. Keep an eye on the layout of your enemy's troops and don't miss an opportunity to send one of your heavy hitters onto a tile occupied by a vulnerable enemy.

Transfer Health

Cost: ○●●●●●
Casters: Adept, Overlord (Demigod and God)
Range: Target creature must be within 7 tiles of caster.

How to Cast:

1. Select spell from Cast menu.
2. Select creature to Transfer Health from.
3. Select creature to Transfer Health to.

Transfer Health allows you to move health energy from any one of your creatures up to seven tiles away to any other friendly creature on the World Map. The spell drains as much health from the donating creature as the recipient needs to achieve full health. If the donating creature doesn't have enough health to fully heal the recipient, the spell only transfers as much health as can be spared from the donor without killing it.

> # Tip
> Transfer Health from creatures that are far from combat to creatures that are on the front lines. If possible, move the donating creature onto a Temple or Citadel after casting the spell so it can recover its own health energy and possibly donate more later in the game.

Transform Land

Cost: ○○●●●●
Casters: Adept, Overlord (Demigod and God)
Range: Target tile must be within five tiles of caster.

How to Cast:
1. Select spell from Cast menu.
2. Select tile to Transform.

Transform Land changes the terrain of a targeted tile into the type that provides the greatest advantage to the caster's creatures. It also transforms all adjacent tiles into terrain of primary or secondary advantage to the caster. Ethereal tiles are immune to this spell.

> ## Tip
> Use Transform Land deep in enemy territory to remove your foes' home field advantage. Select a strategically important tile surrounded by plenty of tiles that don't currently favor your creatures in combat.

PRIMARY AND SECONDARY ADVANTAGE TERRAIN TYPES

Caster's Alignment	Primary Advantage Terrain
Light Order	Sea
Light Chaos	Lava
Dark Order	Plains
Dark Chaos	Dead

Caster's Alignment	Secondary Advantage Terrain
Light Order	Glacier, Swamp
Light Chaos	Mountains, Desert
Dark Order	Mountains, Swamp
Dark Chaos	Glacier, Desert

Wrath

Cost: ◯◯◯●●
Casters: Overlord only (Demigod and God)
Range: Target enemy creature must be within five tiles of caster.

How to Cast:
1. Select your Demigod or God.
2. Select spell from Cast menu.
3. Select target enemy creature.

Wrath is the deadliest spell in the game. It instantly blasts two bars of health out of an enemy creature of your choice within five tiles of the caster. If the creature has two bars of health or less, it is instantly destroyed. This spell is so powerful that only Overlords (Demigods and Gods) can cast it.

> ## Tip
> Using Wrath effectively can weaken a powerful enemy creature so badly that it becomes easy pickings for even the lowliest Sentry. Remember, it cannot be used against creatures on Temples or Citadels. It is best used to weaken a creature, rather than destroy one outright.

WORLD MAPS

WORLD MAP STRUCTURES

wrath
unleashed
chapter 5

world maps
- structures
- terrain
- two-player maps
- three-player maps
- four-player maps

Citadel

Citadels are sanctuaries for Overlords. They are essentially more powerful versions of Temples. Tiles with Citadels on them are immune to magic, whether friendly or hostile, as are any creatures occupying the Citadels.

To occupy a Citadel, move a creature onto it. If a hostile creature already occupies the Citadel, possession goes to the creature that wins the subsequent arena combat.

If one of your creatures occupies a Citadel at the start of your turn, that creature regenerates some health. Citadels provide twice as much health regeneration per turn as do Temples.

If you are playing on a World Map that requires you to occupy a certain number of Temples to win, go for Citadels as well, because they are worth two Temples toward your goal.

Occupying Citadels is also an excellent way to build up your army's Mana. Each Citadel that you occupy gives you 20 percent of a Mana orb per turn.

Gate

Think of Gates as free Teleport spells that any player can take advantage of. Move a creature onto a Gate to instantly transport it to any other Gate of the same color (by pressing the Activate Gate button shown on the screen). If more than two Gates are of the same color, you can choose which one to send the creature through.

A creature may take any movement spaces remaining to it after transporting through a Gate.

Magic Amplifier

A creature occupying a tile containing a Magic Amplifier can cast any spells that an Adept can cast (except Wrath and Resurrect). After leaving the tile containing the Magic Amplifier, the creature can no longer cast spells.

Magic Amplifiers let you cast powerful magic against enemy forces without exposing your Overlord or Adepts to counterattack. Use Magic Amplifiers to your advantage by sending weak creatures onto them and having them cast a Summon Elemental spell against a powerful enemy creature. Or, Teleport one of your heavy hitters directly onto a tile of strategic importance.

Mana Wat

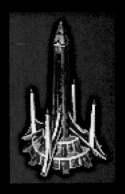

Mana Wats serve one purpose: to produce Mana for the army that occupies them. Move creatures onto Mana Wats to occupy the structures, and you're rewarded with 15 percent of a Mana orb per turn for each Mana Wat that you occupy.

Mana Wats produce more Mana than Temples, but slightly less than Citadels. Remember, though, Mana Wats don't count toward your Temple goal in World Map games that require you to conquer a certain number of Temples to win. In those games, make capturing Mana Wats a secondary concern and focus instead on occupying Temples.

WORLD MAPS

Nexus Point

Nexus Points serve a variety of functions depending on the World Map. To activate Nexus Points, one army's creatures must simultaneously occupy all the Nexus Points. Check the World Map objectives to determine the effect of activating the Nexus Points on that World Map.

Temple

Temples provide Mana, health, and spell immunity; on some World Maps, they are the key to victory. Temples are weaker versions of Citadels, and a World Map always has more Temples than Citadels.

To occupy a Temple, move a creature onto it. If a hostile creature already occupies the Temple, arena combat begins. Possession of the Temple goes to the creature that wins the fight.

Creatures occupying a Temple recover some health at the start of every turn. The amount of health recovered is half as much as the amount provided by a Citadel.

For each Temple that an army occupies, that army earns 10 percent of a Mana orb per turn. Even though Temples provide Mana, they are immune to spells (friendly or hostile), as is the terrain of the tile on which the Temple sits and any creature occupying the Temple.

If the World Map victory conditions require you to capture a certain number of Temples, each Temple that an army occupies counts as one toward the goal. As soon as you occupy the required number of Temples simultaneously, you win the World Map war.

WORLD MAP TERRAIN

Each tile on a World Map represents a Battle Arena of some type of terrain. Each type of terrain (except Ethereal) is aligned with a particular realm or realms. Creatures of those realms have a competitive advantage in the Battle Arena–they suffer half as much damage from Elemental hazards and regenerate magic energy more quickly from Energy Crystals that are aligned with their realm.

> ### Note
> For more information on the Battle Arenas that correspond to the terrain types, see the "Arena Combat Training" section.

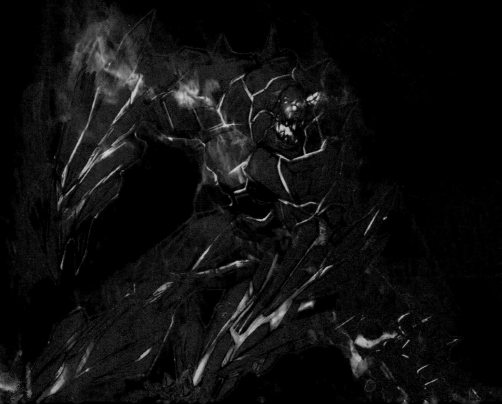

WRATH UNLEASHED
PRIMA'S OFFICIAL STRATEGY GUIDE

TERRAIN REALM ALIGNMENTS

Terrain	Name	Aligned With	Alignment Advantages
	Dead	Dark Chaos	DC suffers 1/2 damage from Elemental hazards and recovers 2x magic energy from their Energy Crystals.
	Desert	Dark Chaos, Light Chaos	DC/LC suffer 1/2 damage from Elemental hazards and recover 1.5x magic from their Energy Crystals.
	Ethereal	None	None
	Glacier	Dark Chaos, Light Order	DC/LO suffer 1/2 damage from Elemental hazards and recover 1.5x magic from their Energy Crystals.
	Lava	Light Chaos	LC suffers 1/2 damage from Elemental hazards and recovers 2x magic from their Energy Crystals.
	Mountain	Dark Order, Light Chaos	DO/LC suffer 1/2 damage from Elemental hazards and recover 1.5x magic from their Energy Crystals.
	Plains	Dark Order	DO suffers 1/2 damage from Elemental hazards and recovers 2x magic from their Energy Crystals.
	Sea	Light Order	LO suffers 1/2 damage from Elemental hazards and recovers 2x magic from their Energy Crystals.
	Swamp	Dark Order, Light Order	DO/LO suffer 1/2 damage from Elemental hazards and recover 1.5x magic from their Energy Crystals.

ENERGY CRYSTAL ALIGNMENTS

Realm	Color of Energy Crystal
Light Order	Blue
Light Chaos	Red
Dark Order	Green
Dark Chaos	Purple

TWO-PLAYER WORLD MAPS

Tip

All the screenshots and World Maps in this section are taken from a Light Order vs. Light Chaos Battle game with default settings. Depending on the settings you have chosen, you may see more or fewer creatures and different terrain in your game, but the structures and layouts of the World Maps will be identical.

Checkered

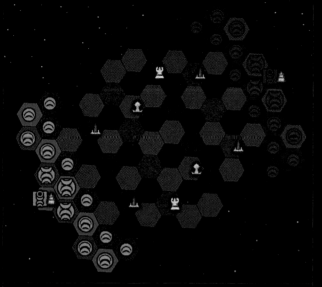

CHECKERED MAP KEY

🛡	Citadel	♜	Temple
	Gate	◎	Sentinel
🔥	Magic Amplifier	◎	Warrior
💧	Mana Wat	✖	Champion
♟	Nexus Point	🏰	Overlord

Difficulty: Intermediate
Temple Total: 6 Points
Need to Win: 6 Points

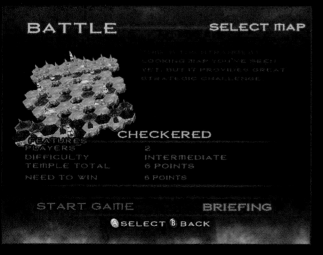

BATTLE — SELECT MAP

CHECKERED

FEATURES
PLAYERS — 2
DIFFICULTY — INTERMEDIATE
TEMPLE TOTAL — 6 POINTS
NEED TO WIN — 6 POINTS

START GAME — BRIEFING

Ⓐ SELECT Ⓑ BACK

Capture six Temple points to win on Checkered.

Checkered is a locked World Map. To unlock it, you must win more than 20 Battle mode wars.

Checkered has one of the most challenging layouts of any World Map, although its difficulty isn't immediately obvious. At the start of the game, it appears as a narrow web of terrain tiles and gaps that drastically limit the movement of non-teleporting creatures.

Tip

Quickly place Sentinel creatures (Centaurs, Unicorns, Centabras, and Dark Unicorns) as close to your opponent's side of the World Map as possible on tiles that have three tiles adjoining. This slows your opponent's advance and allows you to conquer additional Temples and Mana Wats.

TEMPLES

At the start of the game, the World Map contains two Citadels, each occupied by an Overlord and two Temples, for a total of six Temple points. Six Temple points are needed for victory. If the Nexus Points are triggered (see below), an additional two Temples appear, for a total of eight Temple points.

71

wrath
unleashed
chapter 5

world maps
- *structures*
- *terrain*
- *two-player maps*
- *three-player maps*
- *four-player maps*

NEXUS POINTS

Occupy both Nexus Points simultaneously to reveal two more Temples and fill in the gaps with advantageous terrain.

In the center of the World Map are two Nexus Points. If you occupy both of them simultaneously, all the gaps in the map fill in with the terrain that is most advantageous to your realm alignment and two additional Temples appear.

Tip

Your first priority is to capture these Nexus Points. Until the Nexus Points are activated, your opponent can't win without taking your heavily fortified Citadel, which is unlikely.

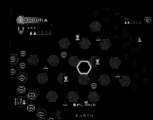

With the gaps filled in to your advantage, move quickly to defeat your enemy.

Trigger the Nexus Points to create a huge terrain advantage for your army, and then take advantage of the now-gapless World Map to fight enemy creatures on terrain that favors your creatures. Make a special effort to capture the two Temples that appear after triggering the Nexus Points, as these are on advantageous terrain.

Collision

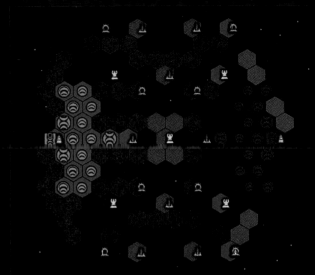

COLLISION MAP KEY

🏛	Citadel	♜	Temple
🔘	Gate	◎	Sentinel
🔺	Magic Amplifier	◎	Warrior
🔻	Mana Wat	◎	Champion
🔱	Nexus Point	🎰	Overlord

Difficulty: Intermediate
Temple Total: 9 Points
Need to Win: 7 Points

BATTLE   SELECT MAP

COLLISION
FEATURES
PLAYERS   2
DIFFICULTY   INTERMEDIATE
TEMPLE TOTAL   9 POINTS
NEED TO WIN   7 POINTS

START GAME   BRIEFING
Ⓐ SELECT Ⓑ BACK

WORLD MAPS

●SWAMP

. WATER+EARTH

Capture seven of the nine Temple points to win on Collision.

There's a reason this World Map is called Collision. It's specifically designed to send both armies' creatures head to head in a clash of combat. You must capture seven of the nine Temple points to win this World Map war, and the best way to do that is to make good use of the Gates scattered around.

TEMPLES

Two Citadels on the World Map are each occupied by an Overlord at the start of the game. The map also has five Temples–two on each army's side of the World Map and one in the center. You must capture seven Temple points to win.

GATES

The four yellow Gates around the perimeter of the World Map are ideal for flanking your enemy.

Collision has eight Gates: four yellow and four blue. The four yellow gates are located around the map perimeter. Move a creature onto any of these Gates to activate it and instantly teleport to any other yellow Gate on the World Map.

Use the yellow Gates to move your creatures down the field of battle quickly and attack deep in enemy territory if your opponent's Citadel is undefended. Remember that the Citadel counts as two Temples toward your Temple point goal.

The yellow Gates are also a big help in moving troops into position to capture the six Mana Wats around the map edges. Although occupying Temples should be your primary goal, it doesn't hurt to snag a Mana Wat or two if you can spare the manpower.

Tip

Note that the yellow Gates closest to your Citadel rest on terrain most favorable to your adversary. The yellow Gates near your opponent's Citadel favor your realm. Occupying the yellow Gates nearest your opponent's Citadel gives you a nice beachhead in enemy territory, cuts off your foe's ability to quickly move to the other end of the map, and gives him or her something else to worry about while you're out capturing Temples.

The four blue Gates are best used to capture the nearby Temples.

The four blue Gates in the center of the World Map work just like the yellow Gates, except that you can use them to transport to the blue Gate of your choice.

At the start of the game, rather than capture the Temples close to the blue Gates on your side of the World Map, use the blue Gates to transport to your opponent's side of the World Map and occupy the Temples on that side. Those Temples sit on terrain that gives your creatures a big advantage in combat.

After capturing the Temples on your opponent's side of the World Map, capture the Temples nearest your Citadel. Defend those Temples with more powerful creatures to offset your terrain disadvantage.

Frenzy

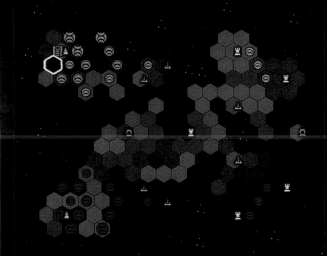

Capture seven of Frenzy's nine Temple points to win.

FRENZY MAP KEY

🏛 Citadel		🏰 Temple	
🚪 Gate		🌀 Sentinel	
🔥 Magic Amplifier		🌀 Warrior	
⚠ Mana Wat		🌀 Champion	
🏛 Nexus Point		🔲 Overlord	

Difficulty: Advanced
Temple Total: 9 Points
Need to Win: 7 Points

Note

Frenzy is a locked World Map. To unlock it, you must complete the second Light Chaos mission.

Frenzy is unique in that both armies' Citadels are on the same side of the World Map, rather than at opposite ends. This mutually vulnerable arrangement is what gives Frenzy its name–it's a mad dash for both armies to occupy Temples while making sure that they don't leave their own Citadels under-defended.

TEMPLES

Occupy the far Temples with Sentinels immediately.

Two Citadels on Frenzy are each occupied by a rival Overlord at the start of the game. There are also five Temples; two pairs are located on the corners of the World Map farthest from the Citadels, and the fifth is in dead center.

Each pair of Temples in the far corners of the map has a trio of creatures of Sentinel rank next to them at the start of the game. Waste no time in securing these two temples with two of your three nearby Sentinels. Position the third between the two Temples for use as a floating defender.

WORLD MAPS

Tip

If the enemy isn't advancing on your pair of Temples, send your floating defender out to occupy the nearby Mana Wat and earn your army some additional Mana.

GATES

The pair of Gates is of extreme strategic importance.

Two Gates are on this World Map. One is between the two Citadels, and the other is between the two pairs of Temples at the far side of the World Map. Once you have secured your pair of Temples, send Sentinels and Warriors through the Gate near your Citadel to mount an attack on your rival's pair of Temples.

Tip

If you can defend the Gate near your Citadel and keep your opponent's creatures from moving through it, you effectively cut your opponent off from the half of the World Map that has all the Temples.

As soon as you can, start moving your most powerful creatures between your opponent's Citadel and the Gate. Not only can you cut off your opponent's access to the Gate, but you can also start massing powerful creatures for an assault on your opponent's Citadel.

Caution

Whatever you do, don't spread your forces too thin. You should have enough creatures on the Temple side of the World Map to defend your pair of Temples and eventually mount an assault on your opponent's Temples. But the Citadel side is more strategically important, because it holds the two Citadels and access to the Gate between them. Don't send too many troops to the Temple side and leave your Overlord and Citadel undefended.

Grandmaster

GRANDMASTER MAP KEY

Citadel		Temple	
Gate		Sentinel	
Magic Amplifier		Warrior	
Mana Wat		Champion	
Nexus Point		Overlord	

Difficulty: Advanced
Temple Total: 9 Points
Need to Win: 7 Points

BATTLE · SELECT MAP

FEATURES
PLAYERS · 2
DIFFICULTY · ADVANCED
TEMPLE TOTAL · 9 POINTS
NEED TO WIN · 7 POINTS

GRANDMASTER

START GAME · BRIEFING

Ⓐ SELECT Ⓑ BACK

Conquer seven of the nine Temple points to emerge victorious on Grandmaster.

Note

Grandmaster is a locked World Map. To unlock it, you must complete the second Dark Chaos mission.

Grandmaster is arranged like a chessboard, with Sentinels as your pawns, Warriors as your rooks and knights, Champions as your bishops, an Adept as your queen, and the Overlord as your king. The World Map is so small that arena combat is guaranteed. Perhaps more than in any other World Map, your arena combat skills are just as important as your strategy, if not more so.

TEMPLES

Two Citadels on Grandmaster are each occupied by an Overlord at the start of the game. The map also has five Temples. Four are in the four corners of the World Map, and creatures (two from each side) occupy all four at the start of the game. A fifth Temple sits in the center of the World Map between two Nexus Points.

Activating the Nexus Points causes two additional Temples to appear (see below). You must capture seven Temple points to win. Because each army occupies four at the start of the game, you can't afford to waste a single move.

Tip

Avoid putting yourself in a position where you must occupy one of your opponent's Temples or Citadel to win. They're usually too well defended. It's better to activate the Nexus Points and capture the three Temples in the center of the World Map instead.

NEXUS POINTS

Occupy both Nexus Points simultaneously to reveal two additional Temples on favorable terrain and a Magic Amplifier.

Without a doubt, your first goal in Grandmaster is to occupy the two Nexus Points in the center of the World Map. When you do, two additional Temples appear next to the Nexus Points on terrain that favors your realm and a Magic Amplifier appears on your side of the World Map.

Move the Nexus Point creatures onto the new Temples as soon as they appear.

As soon as you reveal the additional Temples, move the creatures that activated the Nexus Points onto those Temples. The terrain gives them a huge advantage in defending those Temples. If you have retained control of the four Temple points that you occupied at the start of the game (two Temples and a Citadel), you need only capture one additional Temple to win!

WORLD MAPS

Neutral Zone

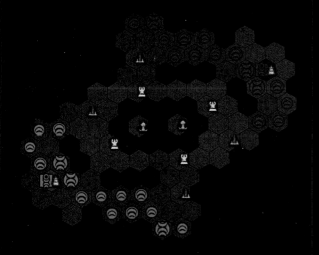

NEUTRAL ZONE MAP KEY

🛡	Citadel	♜	Temple
⌂	Gate	◉	Sentinel
⛰	Magic Amplifier	◎	Warrior
⚠	Mana Wat	⊗	Champion
♟	Nexus Point	🔲	Overlord

Difficulty: Intermediate
Temple Total: 8 Points
Need to Win: 7 Points

Capture seven Temple points to win on Neutral Zone.

Neutral Zone gets its name from the terrain that makes up the World Map. Most of the terrain is Ethereal, which gives no advantage to any realm alignment and resists Transform Land spells.

The rest of the terrain is aligned with the two realms whose creatures are not involved in the current game.

Transform Land spells cast on non-Ethereal terrain can make a big difference in this World Map.

Use your Transform Land spells on non-Ethereal terrain to transform tiles to your advantage. If you can sneak an Adept or Overlord close enough to enemy territory to transform the land near the opposing Citadel, you can weaken their defensive abilities.

TEMPLES

At the start of the game, two Citadels are each controlled by a rival Overlord. Four Temples are in the center of the World Map for a total of eight Temple points. If you simultaneously occupy both Nexus Points (see below), a fifth Temple appears. You must capture seven Temple points to win.

NEXUS POINTS

Occupy both Nexus Points in the center of the World Map to reveal another Temple on advantageous terrain.

If you simultaneously occupy both Nexus Points in the center of the World Map, a fifth Temple appears between them on terrain that favors the army that revealed it.

Make an effort to be the one to reveal the fifth Temple. It is the only Temple that isn't placed on neutral Ethereal terrain, which makes it easier for your army to defend. It also allows you to win the game by occupying your Citadel and all five Temples, rather than having to seize your opponent's Citadel.

Portal Shift

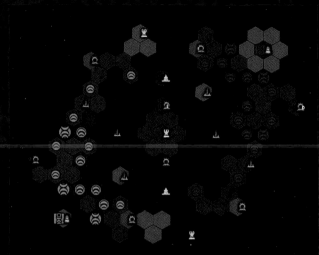

world maps
♦ *structures*
♦ *terrain*
♦ *two-player maps*
♦ *three-player maps*
♦ *four-player maps*

PORTAL SHIFT MAP KEY

🏛	Citadel	♟	Temple
🏚	Gate	◎	Sentinel
🏔	Magic Amplifier	◉	Warrior
🏯	Mana Wat	◍	Champion
🏮	Nexus Point	🎰	Overlord

Difficulty: Advanced
Temple Total: 7 Points
Need to Win: 7 Points

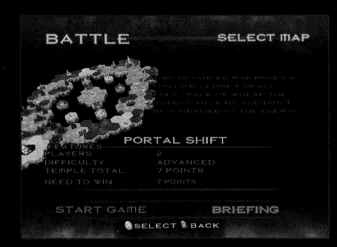

Occupy all seven Temple points to win on Portal Shift.

Portal Shift is an unpredictable World Map with four pairs of Gates and a huge gap in the center. To win, you must move your army quickly and efficiently to every Temple and Citadel, and you must use the Gates effectively to ambush your opponent without getting caught with your pants down.

TEMPLES

Two Citadels on Portal Shift are each occupied by a rival Overlord at the start of the game. The map has three Temples, one in the center and two along the edges. You need seven Temple points to win on Portal Shift, so you must occupy *every single* Temple and Citadel.

GATES

The green and red Gates transport you to the opposite side of the World Map.

Portal Shift has four pairs of gates: red, green, blue, and yellow. Entering any Gate allows you to transport to the other Gate of the same color.

The red and green Gates are on the perimeter of the World Map. Use these Gates to reach the other side of the map quickly. Entering the red Gate on your side of the World Map takes you straight to the one on your opponent's side of the

WORLD MAPS

World Map; the same goes for the green Gates. Use the red and green Gates to ambush the bulk of your opponent's forces and send creatures to occupy your opponent's Citadel.

The yellow and blue Gates go between the center of the World Map and the Citadels.

A yellow or a blue Gate is near each player's Citadel; the paired Gate is on the floating island in the map's center. The yellow and blue Gates are the only way to reach the center of the World Map and the Temple found there.

Tip
The Gate paired with the yellow or blue Gate that is closest to your Citadel sits on terrain that favors your opponent. If you reach the center of the World Map, occupy the yellow or blue Gate that is advantageous to your Realm to prevent your opponent from easily using his or her yellow or blue Gate.

You can also use your yellow or blue Gate to send your creatures all the way across the World Map and ambush your opponent's Citadel. If you're crafty, you can send creatures through the red, green, and yellow or blue Gates and hit your opponent from all sides at once.

Tip
Leave Sentinels near Gates to cut off enemies that might come through them. Even if your opponent sends a powerful creature through, they're held up for at least a turn getting themselves into position to attack your Sentinel.

The Race

THE RACE MAP KEY

Citadel		Temple	
Gate		Sentinel	
Magic Amplifier		Warrior	
Mana Wat		Champion	
Nexus Point		Overlord	

Difficulty: Advanced
Temple Total: 10 Points
Need to Win: 7 Points

Capture seven Temple Points to achieve victory on The Race.

The Race is an extremely challenging World Map for several reasons. The map is broken into six tiny islands, each of which is linked to at least one other island by a Gate. This makes maneuvering quickly almost impossible–you have a limited amount of space on each island, and you must travel through several Gates to reach areas of strategic importance. It's very difficult for walking creatures to move around on this World Map.

The largest of the six islands has three Nexus Points. If you simultaneously occupy all three, you destroy your opponent's Citadel. This sets your opponent back a bit, but it also lowers the number of potential Temple points by two, which means that you must capture all but one Temple to win.

TEMPLES

Two Citadels are on opposite sides of the World Map, each occupied by an Overlord. There are also six Temples–one on each of the two small triangular islands, one on the largest island, and three on the diamond-shaped island between the Citadels. That makes 10 potential Temple points, although you can reduce that number to 8 by destroying your opponent's Citadel with the Nexus Points (see below). You must occupy seven Temple points to win, so every Temple is strategically important.

Tip
It is mathematically possible to win without capturing any of the three Temples on the diamond-shaped island, but that would involve leaving your opponent's Citadel intact and seizing it. Quickly send your troops to that diamond-shaped island; it is strategically vital, and it's also a pain to reach!

GATES

Red and blue Gates link each army's Citadel island with the adjacent triangle-shaped island.

Each army's Citadel island has a single red or blue Gate on it. The other red or blue Gate is on the tiny triangle-shaped island adjacent to the army's Citadel island. The only way to leave your Citadel island (without using a Teleport spell) is to go through that Gate.

Tip
Because the majority of each army's creatures begins on the army's Citadel island, the adjacent triangular islands are of tremendous strategic importance. You can force opponents to fight their way off their own island if you can occupy the Gate that is paired with the one on their Citadel island.

Green and yellow Gates link all four non-Citadel islands.

wrath unleashed chapter 5

world maps
♦ *structures*
♦ *terrain*
♦ *two-player maps*
♦ *three-player maps*
♦ *four-player maps*

80

Yellow and green Gates link one triangle island with the two other large non-Citadel islands. Entering a green or yellow Gate gives you a choice of islands to which to transport. This means that, unless you're planning on using a Teleport spell, you can only reach an island containing Temples if you go through a green or yellow Gate on one of the triangular islands.

NEXUS POINTS

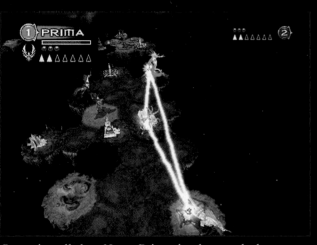

Occupying all three Nexus Points simultaneously destroys your opponent's Citadel.

If you occupy all three Nexus Points on the largest island, your opponent's Citadel is destroyed, which deprives your adversary of the health, Mana, and Temple points that the Citadel provides.

This can be a huge help to you, but it's not necessarily the wisest use of your forces. You're much better off occupying the three Temples on the diamond-shaped island and using your creatures to prevent enemy creatures from coming through onto the two large non-Citadel islands.

If you can keep your opponent pinned down on his own Citadel island and the adjacent triangle island, you can capture seven Temple points and win the game without wasting time on the Nexus Points. Activating the Nexus Points should be a secondary concern if it's a concern at all.

MAGIC AMPLIFIERS

Magic Amplifiers transform the lowliest Sentry into a spell-flinging Adept.

Finally, don't overlook one of the greatest tactical advantages on the World Map–the two Magic Amplifiers, located on the two large non-Citadel islands. Occupying either Magic Amplifier with any creature allows you to cast any spell (except Resurrection and Wrath) anywhere on the island.

Tip
What's the best use of the Magic Amplifiers, you ask? Good question. How about the relatively low-cost Transform Land spell, which can turn half of an island into terrain that gives you the advantage in combat? Or you can Transfer Health from a distant creature on your Citadel island to a creature on the front lines. Binding a powerful enemy also gives you a few rounds to move forces into position and deal with it.

PRIMA'S OFFICIAL STRATEGY GUIDE

Red 5

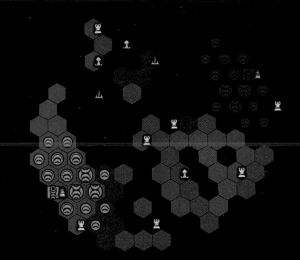

Capture seven Temple Points to achieve victory in Red 5.

wrath
unleashed
chapter 5

world maps
♦ *structures*
♦ *terrain*
♦ *two player maps*
♦ *three-player maps*
♦ *four-player maps*

RED 5 MAP KEY

⛰	Citadel	♜	Temple
⛩	Gate	◎	Sentinel
🔺	Magic Amplifier	◎	Warrior
🔻	Mana Wat	◎	Champion
⬆	Nexus Point	◎	Overlord

Difficulty: Advanced
Temple Total: 11 Points
Need to Win: 7 Points

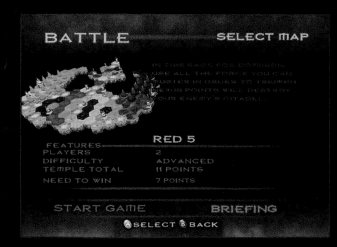

Note

Red 5 is a locked World Map. To unlock it, you must complete the second Light Order mission.

Red 5 is a large map on which all the strategically important points are spread out, so expect to fight a war of multiple fronts. Each half is made up of terrain that favors the army whose Citadel is nearest, making Citadels relatively easy to defend and hard to siege. And if the "rebellious" design of the Red 5 World Map looks familiar to you, just remember that this is a LucasArts game!

TEMPLES

Two Citadels are on opposite sides of Red 5, each occupied by a rival Overlord. Near each Citadel is a Temple, and five additional Temples are in the center of the World Map, bringing the total number of potential Temple points to 11. If you simultaneously capture all three Nexus Points, however, you destroy your opponent's Citadel and reduce the number of potential Temple points to nine. You need seven Temple points to win the game.

Tip

The lone Temple at the tip of the World Map near the two Nexus Points is a pain to walk to, but it's a simple matter for a teleporting creature to cross the gap between friendly territory and the Mana Wat and then skip up to the Temple. You can also position an Adept so that creatures can be Teleported onto that part of the World Map.

WORLD MAPS

NEXUS POINTS

Capture all three Nexus Points to destroy your opponent's Citadel.

Red 5 has three Nexus Points. Two are at the tip of the World Map near the lone Temple and pair of Mana Wats; the third is in the center of the World Map, surrounded by four Temples. Occupy all three Nexus Points at once to blow up your opponent's Citadel and deprive them of the health, Mana, and Temple point benefit that it provides.

Tip

Marching into enemy territory to capture a Citadel and a nearby Temple is tough, especially considering that all the terrain favors the defenders. Better to blow up their Citadel, ignore the Temple near it, and then capture four of the five Temples in the center of the World Map. If you've managed to keep custody of your own Citadel and the Temple next to it, those four additional Temples give you the game!

Seventh

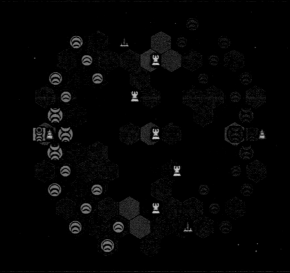

SEVENTH MAP KEY

🛕	Citadel	♜	Temple
🜨	Gate	⊚	Sentinel
🏔	Magic Amplifier	◉	Warrior
⚑	Mana Wat	✖	Champion
♟	Nexus Point	▣	Overlord

Difficulty: Novice
Temple Total: 9 Points
Need to Win: 7 Points

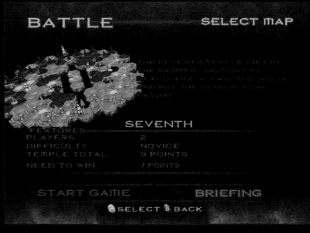

UNLEASHED
PRIMA'S OFFICIAL STRATEGY GUIDE

Capture seven of Seventh's nine Temple points to win.

Seventh is a fairly straightforward World Map that is recommended for novice players to hone their skills on. The World Map gets its name from the Temple in the center of the World Map, which is the seventh structure on the World Map. This strategically important Temple can only be reached via teleportation (see Temples, below).

Aside from that tricky Temple, the map is pretty uncomplicated. The terrain around each Citadel favors the army that controls the Citadel, which means that you won't want to stray too far from your side of the World Map; doing so puts your creatures at a tactical disadvantage.

TEMPLES

The Temple on the small island in the center of the World Map is strategically important.

Two Citadels on Seventh are each occupied at the start of the game by a rival Overlord. In addition to these Citadels, five Temples are located in the middle of the World Map.

One of these Temples appears on a small island in the center of the World Map. It can only be reached by a teleporting creature (Unicorn or Dark Unicorn) or via a Teleport spell.

wrath
unleashed
chapter 5

world maps
◆ structures
◆ terrain
◆ two-player maps
◆ three-player maps
◆ four-player maps

Tip

From your Citadel, your Overlord can Teleport creatures directly onto the center island. You can't Teleport them directly onto the Temple, because it's protected from magic, but send one of your heavy hitters out there immediately to force your opponent into a knock-down, drag-out brawl for possession of the Temple.

The center Temple is on Ethereal terrain, which favors neither player. The four other Temples are on terrain that favors one player over the other. Use your weaker Sentinel creatures to seize the Temples that match your realm's alignment and send your tougher troops to take the Temples on enemy-aligned terrain.

Siphon

SIPHON MAP KEY

🛡	Citadel	♜	Temple
⌂	Gate	◉	Sentinel
⚜	Magic Amplifier	◎	Warrior
⛩	Mana Wat	◍	Champion
🗿	Nexus Point	🎮	Overlord

Difficulty: Advanced
Temple Total: 9 Points
Need to Win: 7 Points

WORLD MAPS

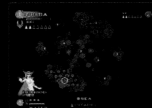

Capture seven of the nine Temple points to conquer Siphon.

Siphon is a snowflake-shaped World Map where the only thing more challenging than beating your opponent in battle might be maneuvering. Both of Siphon's Citadels and four of its five Temples are at the very edges of the World Map, past single-tile land bridges that tend to act as a bottleneck to creatures trying to cross them. Find ways to move quickly and efficiently across Siphon if you want to win.

Tip
Left to their own devices, walking creatures have a great deal of trouble getting to any strategically important area on this World Map. Have your Overlord or Adept (or a creature on a Magic Amplifier) Teleport them past bottlenecks to maximize their abilities.

TEMPLES
Rival Overlords occupy Citadels on opposite sides of the World Map at the start of the game. The map also has five Temples, four on the edges and one in dead center. You must conquer seven of a total of nine potential Temple points to ensure victory.

GATES

Siphon's Gates are the best way to move quickly from one end of the World Map to the other.

Siphon has six Gates: three red and three blue. Each army has one Gate directly in front of its Citadel. The two Gates that are linked to it are at the opposite sides of the map, near two Temples.

Use these Gates to prevent bottlenecking your troops on Siphon's narrow land bridges. They also give you the edge of unpredictability, because any Gate you enter gives you a choice of two destinations.

Tip
One of your first moves should be to send a Sentinel through the Gate near your Citadel. Transport the Sentinel to the Gate nearest the Temple that sits on the terrain favoring your realm alignment, and then capture that Temple. When you go after the Temple near the other Gate, send a more powerful creature, because that Temple is on terrain advantageous to your enemy.

MAGIC AMPLIFIERS

Two Magic Amplifiers are in the middle of the World Map. One creature from each army begins the game near a Magic Amplifier. Use your creature to secure the Magic Amplifier and cast spells against the enemy.

Tip
Summon Elemental is a great spell for taking out or weakening your opponent's most powerful creatures. Teleport can bring reinforcements into the thick of battle in a hurry.

Spellbound

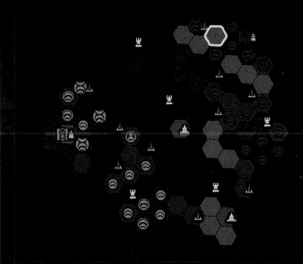

SPELLBOUND MAP KEY

🔺	Citadel	♜	Temple
🔲	Gate	◉	Sentinel
🔥	Magic Amplifier	◎	Warrior
🔺	Mana Wat	◈	Champion
🔺	Nexus Point	🔳	Overlord

Difficulty: Intermediate
Temple Total: 9 Points
Need to Win: 7 Points

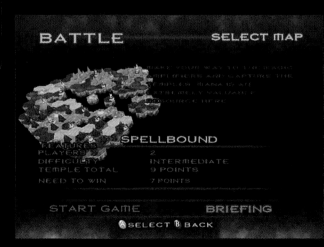

Capture seven of Spellbound's nine Temple points to win.

Capturing Mana Wats is secondary to occupying Temples on most World Maps, but on Spellbound make Mana a priority. Two of the World Map's five Temples are only accessible via teleportation; two centrally located Magic Amplifiers help you put your Mana to good use if you can capture them.

TEMPLES

Reaching this Temple is difficult. Only a Unicorn or Dark Unicorn can do it.

Two Citadels on Spellbound are each initially occupied by a rival Overlord. There are also five Temples–one on each army's side of the World Map, one between the two armies next to a Magic Amplifier, and two on small floating islands between the two armies' Citadels.

One Temple is on a tiny island in the center of the World Map that only a teleporting creature (Unicorn or Dark Unicorn) can reach; you can't use a Teleport spell to reach it, because the Temple protects the tile from magic. Send a teleporting creature out to it early in the game. Also, send another Sentinel past it and onto the enemy's side of the World Map. The terrain there favors your creatures, and you can use your Sentinel as a blocker for any creature seeking to take the Temple from you.

Caution

If you lose all of your Unicorns or Dark Unicorns, you can't reach this Temple, and you can't take it back from an occupying enemy. Of course, if you destroy all of your enemy's Unicorns or Dark Unicorns, your foe can't reach it either!

The Temple on the larger floating island is less of a pain to reach. Either have a teleporter move directly onto it, or cast a Teleport spell to send a creature onto the tiles that surround the Temple.

MANA WATS

Capture nearby Mana Wats as quickly as possible.

Spellbound has a whopping 10 Mana Wats, divided between the two sides of the World Map. If you capture all five on your side of the World Map, as well as the Citadel and the Temple near them, you regenerate more than a full Mana orb every turn. This obviously allows you to be a lot less thrifty with your spell casting, especially if you have creatures on one or both of the Magic Amplifiers.

Taking control of your opponent's Mana Wats is just as important as occupying your own. It adds to your Mana regeneration rate, and subtracts from your opponent's. If you can cast Summon Elemental more often than your opponent can cast Heal, you're at a distinct tactical advantage.

MAGIC AMPLIFIERS

If you can occupy and hold the Magic Amplifiers, you can put all that Mana to good use!

Two Magic Amplifiers are on Spellbound, one on the land bridge between the two armies and one on a tiny floating island next to the tiny island containing the Temple. Conquering and holding these Magic Amplifiers is extremely important on a World Map with as much Mana as Spellbound offers. That Mana won't do you much good if your spell casters are huddled around your Citadel or otherwise not in a good position to use their magical powers.

Tip

Of the two Magic Amplifiers, the one in the center of the World Map is more strategically important. From that Magic Amplifier, a creature can cast Summon Elemental against the bulk of the enemy army, Teleport friendly creatures almost anywhere on the board, and basically make the most of the spells that they're able to cast.

WRATH UNLEASHED
PRIMA'S OFFICIAL STRATEGY GUIDE

Temple Quest

wrath
unleashed
chapter 5

world maps
♦ structures
♦ terrain
♦ two-player maps
♦ three-player maps
♦ four-player maps

TEMPLE QUEST MAP KEY

🔱	Citadel	♟	Temple
🏛	Gate	◎	Sentinel
🔥	Magic Amplifier	◎	Warrior
⚠	Mana Wat	◎	Champion
🔱	Nexus Point	🔟	Overlord

Difficulty: Novice
Temple Total: 10 Points
Need to Win: 7 Points

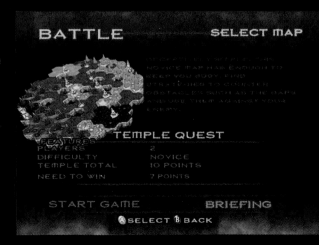

Capture 7 of Temple Quest's 10 Temple points to win.

There's nothing fancy about Temple Quest–it's just one mad dash for Temple points on a small, straightforward World Map. Gaps in the center of the World Map make movement a bit tricky, but you can overcome that with smart use of flying creatures and Teleport spells. Take advantage of the Mana Wats scattered around the World Map as well–Transform Land and Teleport spells are in high demand on Temple Quest.

TEMPLES

Cast Transform Land near Temples that are surrounded by terrain favoring the other army.

Temple Quest's two Citadels are on opposite sides of the World Map, each controlled by a rival Overlord at the start of the game. Between the two Citadels are six Temples, four on terrain that gives one army a fighting advantage over the other.

Make good use of Transform Land spells near Temples that are surrounded by terrain favoring your enemy. You can't transform the tile that the Temple itself sits on (because of the pesky magic protection that Temples provide), but you can lure your opponents into stepping onto terrain that is aligned with your realm, at which point you can leave the Temple and do battle on the advantageous terrain.

War Field

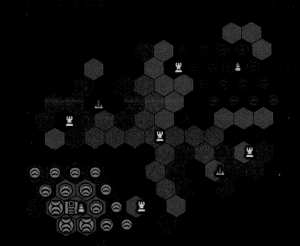

Capture seven of the nine Temple points to emerge victorious from War Field.

War Field is quite possibly the simplest World Map in *Wrath Unleashed*. There are no gaps in the terrain, no Nexus Points to activate, no Gates to pass through. It's just one-on-one combat in a scramble for possession of the Temple points.

Either strategically place Sentinels in the path of your enemy and try to slow your foe down, or just charge straight into battle and let the ground run red with the blood of your adversaries. Both strategies seem to work equally well!

WAR FIELD MAP KEY

🏛	Citadel	♟	Temple
	Gate	🌀	Sentinel
	Magic Amplifier	🌀	Warrior
	Mana Wat		Champion
	Nexus Point		Overlord

Difficulty: Novice
Temple Total: 9 Points
Need to Win: 7 Points

TEMPLES

The Temple in the center of the World Map is pivotal.

Each Overlord starts out the game by occupying one of the two Citadels on either side of the oblong World Map. Between the two Citadels are five Temples.

Four of the Temples are on terrain that favors one army over the other. The fifth Temple is in the dead center of the World Map on Ethereal terrain, which gives neither side an advantage. Capturing the center Temple is essential for victory; if you can't capture it, you must capture the opposing Citadel to win.

THREE-PLAYER WORLD MAPS

Note

All the screenshots and World Maps in this section are taken from a Light Order vs. Light Chaos vs. Dark Order Battle game with default settings. Depending on the settings you choose, you may see more or fewer creatures and different terrain in your game, but the structures and layouts of the World Maps are identical.

*wrath
unleashed
chapter 5*

world maps
- ◆ *structures*
- ◆ *terrain*
- ◆ *two-player maps*
- ◆ *three-player maps*
- ◆ *four-player maps*

Ambush

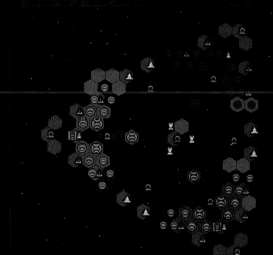

AMBUSH MAP KEY

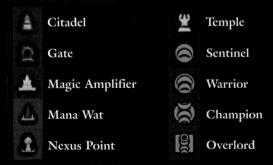

🔺	Citadel	♛	Temple
	Gate	⊚	Sentinel
🔺	Magic Amplifier	⊚	Warrior
△	Mana Wat	⊗	Champion
🔱	Nexus Point	▣	Overlord

Difficulty: Advanced
Temple Total: 9 Points
Need to Win: 5 Points

Capture five of the nine Temple points to win on Ambush.

Ambush is the most complicated three-player Battle World Map in *Wrath Unleashed*. Each army starts on its own large triangular island, which contains a Citadel, two Gates, and two Magic Amplifiers. The trick is to move your forces into the island in the center of the World Map and capture the three Temples there, or use the Gates to sneak up on an opponent from behind and take their Citadel.

TEMPLES

All three Temples are in the center of the World Map.

WORLD MAPS

There are three Citadels in Ambush, each on its own triangular island along the perimeter of the World Map. Each Overlord begins the game occupying one of the Citadels.

Three Temples are in the middle of the World Map, on a triangular island that can only be reached by a teleporting creature, a Teleport spell, or a Gate. You must capture five of the nine potential Temple points to win.

Tip

Competition for the three Temples in the center of the World Map is always intense. You might find it easier to draw your enemies toward the center of the World Map and then ambush their undefended Citadel via a Gate than to capture all three Temples and hold your own Citadel. Adjust your tactics depending on your enemies' movements.

GATES

Green Gates link all four islands.

There are four colors of Gates in Ambush: green, red, blue, and yellow. The four green Gates are found behind each Citadel on the very tips of the World Map and in the center of the World Map between the three Temples. Use the green Gates to move occupying creatures quickly to the center of the World Map to capture the three Temples found there. They also make excellent back doors to your rivals' Citadels.

Caution

Never leave your Citadel or the green Gate behind it undermanned! Doing so invites an enemy to waltz right up to your Citadel and claim its two Temple points. You can't afford that, especially on a World Map that only requires you to have five Temple points for victory!

The paired red, blue, and yellow Gates connect each army's home island to the center island.

The yellow, blue, and red Gates come in pairs. Each army's home island has one of these Gates. The paired Gate is on the center island, on the tile farthest from its mate. These Gates are good for invading the center island, although they don't provide direct access to your opponents' islands.

The red, blue, and yellow Gates have two advantages over the green Gates. First, they're less congested than the green Gates–a lot of arena battles take place on the site of the center green Gate, because that's the one to which everyone wants to transport. Also, the blue, red, and yellow gates aren't as convenient to your adversaries as back doors for ambushes (although you should always be prepared for an enemy to come through one).

MAGIC AMPLIFIERS

Occupy the Magic Amplifiers on your island to attack creatures on rival islands.

Finally, don't neglect the six Magic Amplifiers on the World Map, two of which appear on each army's home island. With 12 Mana Wats up for grabs (four per home island), you can generate an impressive amount of Mana, and the positions of the Magic Amplifiers allow you to attack enemies on their home islands without leaving your own.

PRIMA'S OFFICIAL STRATEGY GUIDE

Nucleus

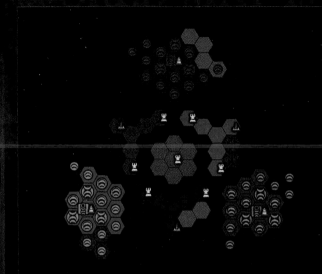

*wrath
unleashed
chapter 5*

world maps
- *structures*
- *terrain*
- *two-player maps*
- *three-player maps*
- *four-player maps*

NUCLEUS MAP KEY

♨	Citadel	♖	Temple
⚱	Gate	◉	Sentinel
⛪	Magic Amplifier	◎	Warrior
⚠	Mana Wat	⊗	Champion
⬆	Nexus Point	▥	Overlord

Difficulty: Novice
Temple Total: 13 Points
Need to Win: 7 Points

Capture 7 of the 13 Temple points in Nucleus to achieve victory.

Nucleus is an ideal World Map for a novice to get an initial three-player Battle game experience. This small, simple World Map doesn't require much in the way of fancy strategy, and it's an excellent way to get used to taking on two enemies at once, or teaming up with another army, or facing two armies simultaneously, depending on how you're playing. Simply capture Temples or destroy enemy Overlords to win. There are no Gates, no Nexus Points, and no Magic Amplifiers to mess with.

TEMPLES

All seven Temples are in the center of the World Map. You need five of them plus your Citadel to win.

Nucleus has three Citadels, and as usual, each is occupied by an Overlord at the start of the game. Seven Temples are in the middle of the World Map, for a grand total of 13 potential Temple points. You need only seven Temple points to win.

The best strategy is to grab the two Temples closest to your own Citadel first. Use some of your strongest creatures, because each Temple sits on terrain that is favorable to one of your opponents.

Next, make a push for the center of the map with moderately strong creatures and seize the central Temple on Ethereal terrain. Finally, move your weaker creatures into position to take the two Temples farthest from your Citadel, as the terrain on those tiles gives your creatures the advantage in combat.

Tip

There are also three Mana Wats, placed between Citadels. Don't waste too much time or energy going for these. Temples provide almost as much Mana and, unlike Mana Wats, they count toward your Temple point goal.

Trinity

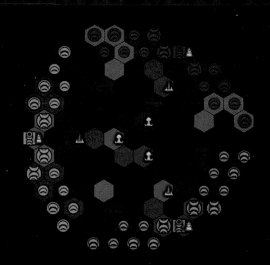

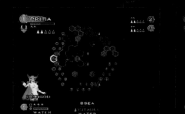

Capture five of the six Temple points to emerge victorious from Trinity.

TRINITY MAP KEY

🔺	Citadel	♖	Temple
🔲	Gate	◉	Sentinel
🔺	Magic Amplifier	◎	Warrior
🔺	Mana Wat	⊗	Champion
🔺	Nexus Point	▣	Overlord

Difficulty: Intermediate
Temple Total: 6 Points
Need to Win: 5 Points

```
BATTLE                    SELECT MAP
...
                 TRINITY
FEATURES
PLAYERS          3
DIFFICULTY       INTERMEDIATE
TEMPLE TOTAL     6 POINTS
NEED TO WIN      5 POINTS

START GAME              BRIEFING
      Ⓐ SELECT Ⓑ BACK
```

Trinity isn't a very confusing World Map, but it can be very frustrating. The center of the World Map is of the greatest strategic value, with the Nexus Points that reveal three additional Temples, but the paths that lead from each army's starting position to the center of the World Map are extremely narrow and prone to bottlenecking.

Tip

Place Sentinels on these pathways to slow down enemy advances. Use teleporting creatures and the Teleport spell to avoid the bottlenecks.

TEMPLES

At the start of the game, there are three Citadels (one for each Overlord) and no Temples. The army that manages to simultaneously activate all three Nexus Points in the center of the World Map reveals three Temples near the Nexus Points.

If no one activates the Nexus Points, you must capture all three Citadels to win the game. If the Nexus Points are activated, you have a bit more leeway. You can capture the three Temples and one Citadel, or two Citadels and one Temple, to win.

NEXUS POINTS

Whoever activates the Nexus Points is halfway to victory.

Occupying all three Nexus Points simultaneously activates them and reveals three Temples on terrain that exclusively favors the army that activated the Nexus Points. Activating the Nexus Points also reveals a Mana Wat on similarly aligned terrain in the center of the World Map.

If you reveal the Temples, you're halfway to winning the game. You have at least three creatures near three Temples on your home turf; if you can occupy those three Temples and hold your own Citadel, you win. Activating the Nexus Points should be your primary concern at the start of the game.

Triple Play

world maps
- *structures*
- *terrain*
- *two-player maps*
- *three-player maps*
- *four-player maps*

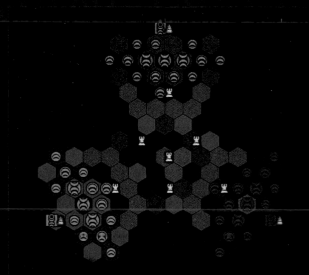

TRIPLE PLAY MAP KEY

🏛	Citadel	♖	Temple
⌂	Gate	◉	Sentinel
🔺	Magic Amplifier	◉	Warrior
🔺	Mana Wat	◉	Champion
🔱	Nexus Point	▣	Overlord

Difficulty: Novice
Temple Total: 13 Points
Need to Win: 7 Points

Capture 7 of the 13 Temple points to win on Triple Play.

Triple Play is a straight-forward World Map, with no Nexus Points, Gates, or Magic Amplifiers to worry about. Just head for the center of the World Map and snag five Temples to go with your Citadel, and you win.

Tip
You can effectively seal off your Citadel from attack by placing creatures between the gaps near the center of the World Map. Also, use Sentinels to create barriers that slow down your enemy's advances.

TEMPLES

Move your creatures to the center of the World Map as quickly as possible to capture Temples.

At the start of the game, each army occupies one Citadel and one Temple, for a total of three Temple points each. Four unoccupied Temples are in the center of the World Map, making 13 potential Temple points up for grabs.

Tip
The easiest way to win is to retain control of your Citadel and Temple and capture the four Temples in the center of the World Map.

WORLD MAPS

FOUR-PLAYER MAPS

Note
All the screenshots and World Maps in this section are taken from a Light Order vs. Light Chaos vs. Dark Order vs. Dark Chaos Battle game with default settings. Depending on the settings you choose, you may see more or fewer creatures and different terrain in your game, but the structures and layouts of the World Maps are identical.

Death Star

DEATH STAR MAP KEY

Icon	Name	Icon	Name
	Citadel		Temple
	Gate		Sentinel
	Magic Amplifier		Warrior
	Mana Wat		Champion
	Nexus Point		Overlord

Difficulty: Intermediate
Temple Total: 9 Points
Need to Win: 7 Points

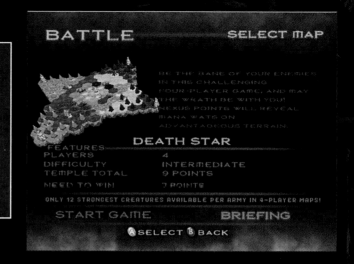

BATTLE   SELECT MAP

DEATH STAR
FEATURES
PLAYERS   4
DIFFICULTY   INTERMEDIATE
TEMPLE TOTAL   9 POINTS
NEED TO WIN   7 POINTS

ONLY 12 STRONGEST CREATURES AVAILABLE PER ARMY IN 4-PLAYER MAPS!

START GAME   BRIEFING

SELECT BACK

Capture seven of the nine Temple points to conquer Death Star.

Death Star is a four-player Battle World Map with a simple layout that is designed to provoke earth-shaking battles. This four-pointed World Map is so small that you won't be able to stay out of arena combat for long. Charge for the center, activate the Nexus Points, and occupy the Temples to emerge victorious.

TEMPLES

At the start of the game, each army occupies one Citadel. A lone Temple sits in the middle of the World Map, for a grand total of nine potential Temple points. You must possess seven Temple Points to win the game.

Activating the Nexus Points reveals four more Temples on advantageous terrain. If no one activates the Nexus Points, you must conquer three of the four Citadels, plus the lone Temple, to win. If you do activate the Nexus Points, you can achieve victory by occupying only your own Citadel and the five Temples, rather than fight your way through the enemy ranks to capture their Citadels.

*wrath
unleashed
chapter 5*

world maps
◆ *structures*
◆ *terrain*
◆ *two-player maps*
◆ *three-player maps*
◆ *four-player maps*

NEXUS POINTS

Whoever activates the Nexus Points gains a huge tactical advantage.

Activating the two Nexus Points in the center of the World Map fills in the four nearby gaps with Temples on terrain that favors the army that activated the switches. This is a huge advantage, as the additional Temples allow you to win the game without having to occupy any rival Citadels.

Tip

Make the Nexus Points your first priority on Death Star. If you can trigger them, you cause four easily defended Temples to appear.

Mana Flux

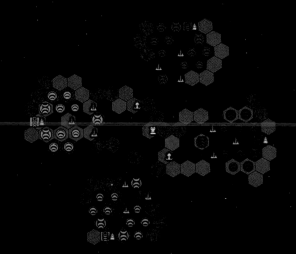

MANA FLUX MAP KEY

🏛	Citadel	♛	Temple
🏛	Gate	◉	Sentinel
🏛	Magic Amplifier	◉	Warrior
🏛	Mana Wat	◎	Champion
🏛	Nexus Point	▣	Overlord

Difficulty: Intermediate
Temple Total: 9 Points
Need to Win: 7 Points

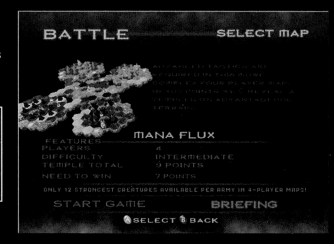

WORLD MAPS

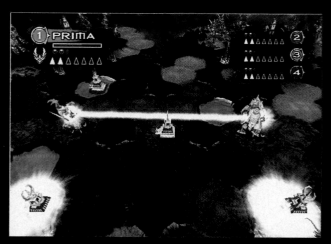

Occupy seven of the nine Temple points to win on Mana Flux.

Mana Flux is similar to Death Star: A four-player World Map has a lone Temple and two Nexus Points that reveal four more Temples on terrain advantageous to the army that reveals them.

However, unlike Death Star, Mana Flux also has 12 Mana Wats (3 near each Citadel), which gives Overlords and Adepts a big Mana boost–and the World Map its name. Mana Flux is also dotted with more than a dozen gaps, which makes movement tricky, particularly for walking creatures.

Tip

Use your Sentinels to block enemy advances on narrow pathways. Force your foes to fight on terrain that puts them at a disadvantage. And don't forget to occupy Mana Wats to juice up your Mana supply.

TEMPLES

At the start of the game, four Citadels are each occupied by an Overlord, and a single Temple sits in the middle of the World Map. If you don't activate the Nexus Points (which reveal four additional Temples), you must capture two other Citadels, keep possession of your own, and take the lone Temple to win.

Activating the Nexus Points causes four Temples to appear in the center of the map on advantageous terrain. These Temples are located near each army's Citadel, so it's still tricky to conquer them all, but at least the terrain gives you an advantage (if you were the one who activated the Nexus Points).

NEXUS POINTS

Triggering the Nexus Points reveals four Temples on advantageous terrain.

As on Death Star, your primary goal at the start of the game is to reach and occupy both Nexus Points simultaneously. Doing so reveals four additional Temples on terrain that gives your armies a huge advantage in combat.

Quad

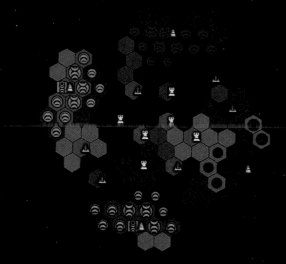

Capture half of the 14 potential Temple points to win on Quad.

Quad might be the simplest four-player World Map in *Wrath Unleashed*, but that doesn't mean it's easy. Although there are no Nexus Points, Gates, or Magic Amplifiers, you must still occupy Temples and Mana Wats and defend them against three other armies. Use the usual World Map strategies (use Sentinels as blockers, teleport around gaps to save time, go for Temples first and Mana Wats second), and you'll find that Quad can be an excellent four-player Battle learning experience.

TEMPLES

All the Temples are clustered in the center of the World Map.

In addition to the four Citadels that the Overlords occupy at the start of the game, the World Map has six Temples in the center. To win, you must occupy seven Temple points simultaneously, which means you must hold one Citadel and five Temples, two Citadels and three Temples, three Citadels and a Temple, or four Citadels. The first goal is the easiest to achieve; they just get tougher from there.

wrath unleashed chapter 5

world maps
- *structures*
- *terrain*
- *two-player maps*
- *three-player maps*
- *four-player maps*

QUAD MAP KEY

🏰	Citadel	♜	Temple
⛩	Gate	◉	Sentinel
🔺	Magic Amplifier	◉	Warrior
🔺	Mana Wat	◉	Champion
🔺	Nexus Point	🔲	Overlord

Difficulty: Novice
Temple Total: 14 Points
Need to Win: 7 Points

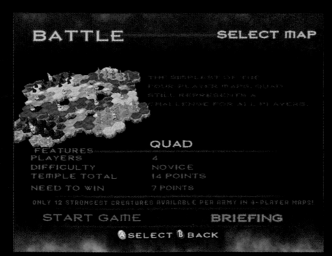

BATTLE   SELECT MAP

QUAD

FEATURES
PLAYERS   4
DIFFICULTY   NOVICE
TEMPLE TOTAL 14 POINTS
NEED TO WIN   7 POINTS

ONLY 12 STRONGEST CREATURES AVAILABLE PER ARMY IN 4-PLAYER MAPS!

START GAME   BRIEFING

Ⓐ SELECT Ⓑ BACK

Tip

Set your sights on capturing Temples that sit on terrain that favors your troops, and expand from there.

Trailblazer

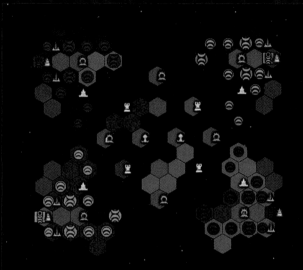

TRAILBLAZER MAP KEY

🜋	Citadel	♖	Temple
🜊	Gate	🜖	Sentinel
🜍	Magic Amplifier	🜖	Warrior
🜁	Mana Wat	🜖	Champion
🜂	Nexus Point	🜖	Overlord

Difficulty: Advanced
Temple Total: 12 Points
Need to Win: 7 Points

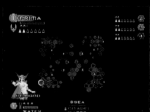

Capture 7 of the 12 Temple points to conquer Trailblazer.

Trailblazer is the most complex four-player World Map in *Wrath Unleashed*. Each army begins on a small floating island with a Citadel, two Mana Wats, a Gate, and a Magic Amplifier. In the center of the World Map are four Temples and two Nexus Points that create a bridge to the island of the army that activates them.

There's a lot going on in this World Map. You must watch out for sneak attacks on your home island from Gate-using enemies, reach the Nexus Points before any other opponent does, and acquire and use Mana effectively through your Mana Wats and Magic Amplifier. Our advice is to make sure that your Citadel is secure at all times, and then focus on activating the Nexus Points. Once you do that, your battle is half won; just focus on winning arena battles and conquering Temples.

TEMPLES

At the start of the game, each Overlord occupies a Citadel. Four additional Temples are on the World Map's center island, for a grand total of 12 Temple points. You need seven Temple points to win.

To reach the center island, you must use a Unicorn or Dark Unicorn, a Teleport spell, or a Gate. If you activate the Nexus Points in the center of the World Map, a fifth Temple appears on terrain advantageous to your army.

wrath unleashed chapter 5

world maps
- *structures*
- *terrain*
- *two-player maps*
- *three-player maps*
- *four-player maps*

Tip

Conquering the five Temples and holding your own Citadel is the easiest way to win. Be the one to activate the Nexus Points and storm across to the center island to take those Temples!

NEXUS POINTS

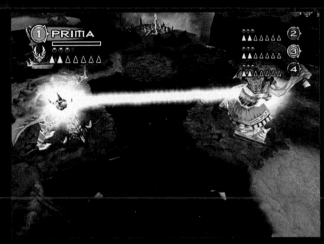

Occupy both Nexus Points simultaneously to create a land bridge between your island and the center island and reveal a fifth Temple.

Activating the two Nexus Points in the center of the World Map gives you a couple of huge advantages over your opponents. First, it creates a fifth Temple on friendly terrain in the center of the World Map. This makes it possible to win the game by occupying only one Citadel in addition to the five Temples on the center island.

More important, it also creates a land bridge between your home island and the center island, where all the Temples are. This makes it much easier to move troops onto the center island and take possession of the Temples.

Caution

If you trigger the Nexus Points and create the land bridge, don't overcommit your creatures to the center island. Remember that your own Citadel is vulnerable to attack from an enemy who comes through the Gate two tiles away from it.

GATES

Red Gates link Player 1's island, Player 2's island, and the center island.

Yellow Gates link Player 3's island, Player 4's island, and the center island.

The arrangement of the Gates in Trailblazer is either a big help or a huge vulnerability, depending on how you have arranged the teams of players. There are three red Gates, one on Player 1's island, one on Player 2's island, and one on the center island near Player 3 and 4's islands. There are also three yellow Gates, one on Player 3's island, one on Player 4's island, and one on the center island.

If Players 1 and 2 or 3 and 4 are on a team together, this arrangement is a great advantage, because their troops can quickly move to reinforce each other's home islands. If Players 1 and 2 or 3 and 4 are adversaries, however, they have very convenient back doors to each other's home island. Depending on whether or not you can trust your Gate partner, you may need to keep your home island's Gate heavily reinforced.

Caution

Even if you and your Gate partner are allied, remember that your opponents can still sneak in through the third Gate, located on the center island.

Blue Gates take you from one side of the center island to the other.

The blue Gates, on the other hand, aren't as tactically significant. They simply transport creatures from one side of the center island to the other. This can be a help when you need to quickly attack or reinforce Temples, but it's not nearly as deserving of your attention as the red and yellow Gate situation.

MAGIC AMPLIFIERS

Magic Amplifiers let you work your magic on neighboring islands without exposing yourself to the risk of traveling to them.

Last but certainly not least, don't overlook the Magic Amplifier on your home island. Place a creature on one to create a simple way to Teleport creatures to and from the center island or your neighbor's home island or attack distant creatures with a Summon Elemental spell. You'll find that the Magic Amplifier, used in conjunction with the two Mana Wats on your home island, is a crucial addition to your war chest.

PRIMA'S OFFICIAL STRATEGY GUIDE

ARENA COMBAT TRAINING

wrath unleashed chapter 6

arena combat training
- ◆ *arena combat*
- ◆ *arenas*

ARENA COMBAT

Positioning your creatures strategically on the World Map is only half of what it takes to succeed in *Wrath Unleashed*. If you want to seize territory from your opponent, you have to fight for it in arena combat. After playing through Tutorial mode, read this section of the guide thoroughly to learn the advanced techniques that elevate you to Godhood.

Terrain

Generally speaking, when two creatures face off in arena combat, the creature with more health energy is favored. But the terrain on which they fight can give a big advantage to one of the creatures. An underdog can pull off an upset, or a favored creature can put down a smaller rival without suffering a scratch.

Each realm's creatures are affiliated with a certain element, and every terrain type (except ethereal terrain) is also affiliated with one or two elements. Creatures affiliated with the same element as the terrain gain advantages when fighting on that terrain, such as faster magic energy regeneration from Energy Crystals and less susceptibility to damage from environmental hazards.

ELEMENTAL AFFILIATIONS

Element	Affiliated Realm	Affiliated Terrain*
Earth	Dark Order (Durlock)	**Plains**, Mountains, Swamp
Fire	Light Chaos (Epothos)	Desert, **Lava**, Mountains
Water	Light Order (Aenna)	Glacier, **Sea**, Swamp
Wind	Dark Chaos (Helamis)	**Dead**, Desert, Glacier
None	n/a	Ethereal

*Terrain in **boldface** is exclusively advantageous to that realm's creatures. No other realm's creatures get any advantage whatsoever from that terrain.

Health and Magic

The lower left corner of the screen shows the selected creature's health on the World Map.

When you move the cursor over a creature on the World Map, its health meter appears in the lower left corner of the screen. The horizontal red bar represents the creature's current health; the red orbs above it represent reserve health bars. If the creature's health bar is depleted, one of the reserve health orbs disappears and the bar is refilled. If the creature's health bar is depleted and it has no reserve health orbs, the creature is killed.

In combat, the red bar in the corner of the screen is the creature's health. The blue bar is its magic energy.

102

ARENA COMBAT TRAINING

In arena combat, a red bar in the upper corner of the screen represents a creature's health energy. The attacking creature's health is shown in the upper left corner, and the defending creature's health is in the upper right corner. Reserve health orbs are represented by red dots above the health bars.

A blue bar under the health bar represents the creature's magic energy. Every magic attack that the creature uses (heavy magic, light magic, or special magic) depletes some of its magic energy. Reserve magic energy orbs are represented by the blue dots below the magic energy bar. You can replenish your creature's magic energy by standing next to an Energy Crystal.

Note
Your creature does not regenerate any health energy after a battle unless it occupies a Citadel or Temple. This means that a strong creature can be worn down and defeated by several smaller creatures. A creature's magic energy, on the other hand, is fully refilled before every fight.

Combo Attacks

Link together combinations of light and heavy melee attacks to inflict greater damage.

In melee combat, you have a much better chance of defeating an opponent if you use combinations of light and heavy melee attacks (combos). Timing is essential when executing combo attacks–as your first attack hits your opponent, press the next attack button to execute the second attack in the combo. Your opponent tries to block or dodge your combo attacks, but if you know what you're doing, it gets harder and harder to interrupt a combo once it gets rolling.

The table lists generic combo attacks that any creature can execute. The particular attacks vary, but these button presses all result in combos.

GENERIC COMBO ATTACKS

Buttons*	Notes
LLL	-
LLH	-
LH	-
HH	-
HLL	The second and third swings are the same as for LLL.
HLH	The second and third swings are the same as for LLH.

* "L" stands for light melee attack and "H" stands for heavy melee attack.

Tip
Never come at your opponent with a single melee attack. You inflict only a small amount of damage and set yourself up for a brutal counterattack. Always try to execute a combo.

PRIMA'S OFFICIAL STRATEGY GUIDE

wrath
unleashed
chapter 6

arena combat training

◆ arena combat
◆ arenas

SIGNATURE ATTACKS

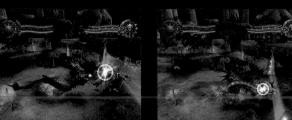

A creature's signature attack is its most powerful melee attack, period.

In addition to its generic combos, each creature also has its own signature attack, which is a combo attack of tremendous power. Signature attacks are tricky to pull off, especially since they vary from creature to creature. But knowing how to execute them separates the *Wrath Unleashed* masters from the talented amateurs.

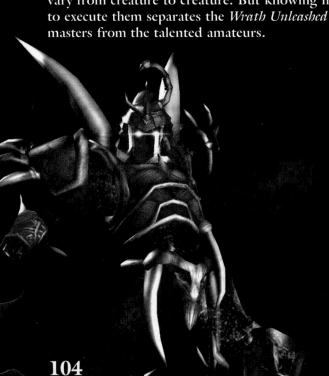

SIGNATURE ATTACK QUICK REFERENCE

Creature*	Buttons**	Attack
LO Centaur	LLLH (D)	Back Kick
LO Unicorn	LLHH	Mystic Hoof Stomp
LO Giantess	LLLH	Hammer Sweep
LO Genie	LLHH (D)	Whirling Blade
LO Water Elemental	LLLH	Impact Wave
LO Juggernaut Adept	LLLH	Force Sword
LO Frost Dragon	LLLH (D)	Tunneling Tail Attack
LO Ogre Mage	LLHH	Phantom Blade
LO Demigod	LLLH (D)	Ice Wall
LO God	LLLH (D)	Energy Nova
LC Centaur	LLLH (D)	Back Kick
LC Unicorn	LLHH	Mystic Hoof Stomp
LC Giantess	LLHH (D)	Hammer Sweep
LC Genie	LLLH	1000 Whirlwinds
LC Fire Elemental	LLLH	Impact Wave
LC Juggernaut Adept	LLLH	Magic Wave Attack
LC Blaze Dragon	LLLH (D)	Scorpion Stinger
LC Fire Giant	LLLH	Cannonball
LC Demigod	LLLH (D)	Pole Vault Smash
LC God	LLLH (D)	Fire Storm Whirlwind
DO Centabra	LLHH (D)	Back Kick
DO Dark Unicorn	LLLH (D)	Energy Bolt
DO Spirit Armor	LLLH	Whirling Uppercut
DO Djinn	LLHH (D)	Whirling Blade
DO Earth Elemental	LLHH (D)	Elemental Twister
DO Nightmare Adept	LLHH (D)	Adept Energy Slash

ARENA COMBAT TRAINING

DO Arch Demon	LLLH	Dual Wing Slam
DO Iron Golem	LLLH (D)	Flying Iron Crash
DO Demigod	LLLH	Staff Slam Spikes
DO God	LLLH	Earth Wall Summon
D Centabra	LLHH (D)	Back Kick
DC Dark Unicorn	LLLH (D)	Energy Bolt
DC Spirit Armor	LLLH (D)	Energy Expand Blast
DC Djinn	LLLH	1000 Whirlwinds
DC Wind Elemental	LLHH (D)	Elemental Twister
DC Nightmare Adept	LLLH	Whirlwind Hooves
DC Chaos Demon	LLHH	Double Energy Blast
DC Cyclops	LLLH (D)	Rolling Claw Smash
D Demigod	LLLH (D)	Kiss of Death
DC God	LLLH (D)	Staff Seduction Blast

* LO is Light Order, LC is Light Chaos, DO is Dark order, and DC is Dark Chaos.

** (D) means that the signature attack is a *dash attack*, which must be performed while the creature is running. All other signature attacks are performed when the creature is standing still.

Magic

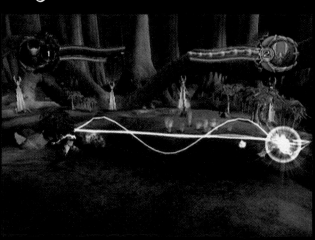

Know your creatures' spells and use them to supplement your melee attacks.

Every creature also has three magic attacks: a light magic attack, a heavy magic attack, and a special magic attack. Each creature has its own set of spells. Knowing what they are and how to use them makes a huge difference in combat (refer to the "Overlords and Creatures" section of this guide for more information on each creature's spells).

A creature can use its magic in arena combat only if it has magic energy. Keep an eye on your magic meter. If it gets too low, move to an Energy Crystal to replenish your magic energy so you don't have to depend solely on melee attacks.

Tip

Most creatures have at least one ranged magic attack. Use it as many times as possible at the start of combat to soften up your enemy, and use it whenever there's enough distance between you and your foe to press the attack without leaving yourself open to retaliation.

Blocking

Mastering the subtle science of blocking is essential if you want to conquer the Shattered Realms.

Unleashing attack after attack by mashing buttons is enough to take out foes of average skill, but *Wrath Unleashed* masters just block your attacks and hit you with a counterattack combo.

Practice blocking and counterattacking in the Versus mode. As soon as you block an enemy's attack, release the Block button and hit your foe with a combo attack that begins with a quick light melee attack. Blocking an attack and counterattacking beats waiting for an enemy to drop its guard, because every creature is vulnerable to counterattack immediately after making an unsuccessful attack.

Tip

You can't block magic attacks. The only way to avoid a magic attack is to dodge it or use the Magic Shield, Dive, or Blink spells, if your creature has them.

Strafing and Dodging

Environmental Features

Block and move to strafe and dodge out of the way of your opponent's attacks.

You can move around the arena while holding down the Block button. This is called strafing, and it's another advanced technique that you should practice in Versus mode. When strafing, your creature faces your opponent, no matter where either of you moves.

Strafing is great for keeping distance between you and your foe without having to turn away from them. You can release the Block button to fire off some fast ranged magic attacks and quickly return to strafing.

Strafing is also excellent for dodging the first attack of a combo attack and then coming in with a combo counterattack. Strafing isn't as fast as regular movement, but it's much more useful in combat.

Tip
Like blocking, the only way to truly master strafing is to practice. Set up a 120-second Versus match and strafe and block all your opponent's attacks without counterattacking. When you can do this with a Sentinel, you've mastered the skill.

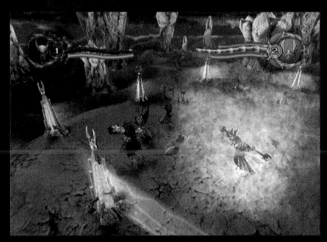

Environmental features often inflict damage on creatures that blunder into them.

Another important factor to consider when fighting in arena combat are environmental features. These range from innocuous rocks and trees to deadly tornados, Death Spikes, and Lightning Strikes.

Familiarize yourself with each arena and learn to recognize the environmental features. You should be able to tell at a glance the difference between an Energy Crystal, which refills your magic energy, and a Lightning Pylon, which sends a bolt of electricity through you if you're careless.

Lure your opponents to environmental hazards and use them to your advantage. Don't forget that environmental hazards do less damage to creatures aligned with the terrain. For instance, if you're controlling a Light Order army and you're fighting on sea terrain, you won't suffer nearly as much damage from Solar Strikes or Death Spikes in that arena as your opponent will.

Tip
If you're outmatched in a fight but have the terrain on your side, dodge your opponent's attacks and use the environmental features against them by luring them into water or quicksand to slow them down, or trick them into standing on Death Spikes or near Exploding Rocks.

ARENA COMBAT TRAINING

ARENAS

There are 11 arenas in *Wrath Unleashed*. Nine correspond to terrain types found on World Maps (dead, desert, ethereal, glacier, lava, mountain, plains, sea, and swamp). Any battle initiated on a World Map terrain tile takes place in the corresponding arena.

Two locked arenas, Elephant Pool and Metal Age, appear only in Versus and Team Fighter games. These are not aligned with any particular element, and they have no environmental features.

Note

In the following descriptions, "Elemental Features" means features of the arena that are of greater benefit to creatures aligned with the arena. "Neutral Features" are environmental features that offer no advantage or disadvantage for any creature, regardless of elemental alignment.

Dead

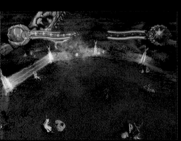

Aligned Realm(s):
Dark Chaos

Elemental Features: Lightning Tornado, Lightning Strikes, Lightning Pylons, Energy Crystal, Death Spikes
Neutral Features: Corrupted boulder, rock outcrop, tree

Dead terrain is a barren, lifeless wasteland that shows the scars suffered from exposure to the harshest elements. Lightning Tornadoes sweep up creatures and inflict massive amounts of damage upon them. Lightning Strikes rain down from the sky, and Lightning Pylons wait to zap any creature foolish enough to stand between them. You also have to worry about the patches of Death Spikes that pop up out of the ground to impale any creatures standing on them.

Various neutral obstacles, such as corrupted boulders, rock outcrops, and trees, block your ranged magic attacks and hinder your evasive maneuvers.

Dark Chaos creatures are naturally resistant to the hazards of dead terrain and suffer significantly less damage than creatures of any other realm alignment. Dark Chaos creatures also regenerate magic energy twice as quickly as any other Realm's creature when they stand near Energy Crystals in dead terrain.

Desert

Aligned Realm(s):
Dark Chaos,
Light Chaos

Elemental Features: Sandstorm, quicksand, Energy Crystal, Death Spikes
Neutral Features: Boulder, rock outcrop

Desert terrain is a blend of Fire and Wind elements and favors Dark and Light Chaos realm alignments. Creatures aligned with Dark Chaos or Light Chaos suffer only half-damage from a desert's whirling sandstorms or vicious Death Spikes.

Desert terrain also has pools of quicksand that slow down any Light or Dark Order creature that runs through them. Light and Dark Chaos creatures are not slowed by quicksand, and they also regenerate combat magic energy one and a half times as quickly when near Energy Crystals of their own alignment. Red Energy Crystals are aligned with Light Chaos, and purple Energy Crystals are aligned with Dark Chaos.

Watch out for the boulders and rock outcrops that litter the desert landscape. Although they won't injure you, these obstacles can block your attacks and limit your mobility.

Elephant Pool

Aligned Realm(s):
None
Elemental Features:
None
Neutral Features:
None

Note

Elephant Pool is a locked arena. To unlock it, win more than 20 Team Fighter games. Elephant Pool never appears as a Battle or Campaign mode arena; it only shows up in Team Fighter or Versus mode.

wrath unleashed chapter 6

arena combat training
• *arena combat*
• *arenas*

Elephant Pool is a vast arena with no environmental features–no spikes jutting from the ground, no magic blasts raining from the sky, and no trees or rocks to hide behind. The arena forces you into one-on-one combat on an even playing field, where only your fighting prowess matters.

Because there are no environmental features, it's impossible to recover your magic energy during battle–there are no Energy Crystals! There also aren't any boulders lying around the arena, which rules out the use of the Grab & Throw magic attack.

Ethereal

Aligned Realm(s):
None
Elemental Features: None
Neutral Features:
Ethereal Strike, Teleporter Vortex, Ethereal Rift, Energy Crystal, Ethereal Mass

Ethereal terrain is a product of pure magical forces, and it favors no realm over any other. All creatures regenerate magic energy at the same rate when standing near Energy Crystals, and environmental hazards do the same amount of damage to all creatures.

The only hazards you have to worry about are the unpredictable Ethereal Strikes that rain from the sky. Watch for a pulsing circle of energy to appear on the ground–that's where the Ethereal Strike will hit.

Teleporter Vortexes and Ethereal Rifts won't hurt you, but they make combat a bit trickier. The Vortexes randomly redirect magic and melee attacks, and the Rifts randomly teleport creatures across the Battle Arena.

Finally, use the Ethereal Masses to your advantage. These environmental obstacles can be used as cover against physical or magical attacks–although they can block your attacks as well.

Glacier

Aligned Realm(s):
Dark Chaos, Light Order

Elemental Features: Snow Pit, snowstorm, Energy Crystal, Death Spikes
Neutral Features: Boulder, ice outcrop, tree

Dark Chaos and Light Order creatures don't have as much to fear from Glacier terrain's whirling snowstorms or Death Spikes, but other creatures suffer twice as much damage from these icy hazards. Dark Chaos and Light Order creatures regenerate battle magic energy one and a half times as fast as other creatures when standing next to an Energy Crystal of their realm's alignment. Dark Chaos Energy Crystals are purple, and Light Order Energy Crystals are blue.

Dark Order and Light Chaos creatures are also slowed down by Snow Pits, while Dark Chaos and Light Order creatures can easily charge through them.

Glacier's environmental obstacles include boulders, ice outcrops, and trees, all of which can be used to block magic or melee attacks. Don't get cornered in them!

ARENA COMBAT TRAINING

Lava

Aligned Realm(s):
Light Chaos

Elemental Features: Lava Pool, Fire Vent, Fireball, Energy Crystal, Death Spikes
Neutral Features: Boulder, rock outcrop

Lava terrain oozes with molten magma that threatens to engulf creatures other than those of the Light Chaos realm. Light Chaos creatures suffer minimal damage from immersion in Lava Pools or exposure to steaming Fire Vents, razor-sharp Death Spikes, and explosive Fireballs.

Light Chaos creatures also regenerate combat magic energy twice as fast as any other creatures when they stand next to Energy Crystals.

Most of the environmental features of lava terrain are deadly. But a few boulders and rock outcrops scattered around the arena can be used as cover against magic and melee attacks.

Metal Age

Aligned Realm(s):
None
Elemental Features:
None
Neutral Features:
None

Note

Metal Age is a locked arena. To unlock it, win more than 100 arena matches. Metal Age is not aligned with any order, so you'll never see it in Campaign or Battle games; it appears only in Versus and Team Fighter modes.

Like Elephant Pool, Metal Age is a featureless arena where only your combat skills help you survive. You can't count on any environmental hazards or elemental affiliation to pull your fat out of the fire!

Because there are no Energy Crystals in the arena, you can't replenish your magic energy. You also can't use the Grab & Throw spell, because there are no boulders to pick up and hurl.

The most dangerous areas of Metal Age are the L-shaped corners at one end of the arena. If an opponent backs you into one, it's very hard to escape without using Blink or Dive magic.

Mountain

Aligned Realm(s):
Dark Order,
Light Chaos

Elemental Features: Scorched Earth, Exploding Rocks, Energy Crystal, Death Spikes
Neutral Features: Boulder, rock outcrop, tree

This rough terrain is extremely inhospitable to creatures from the Dark Chaos and Light Order realms. Exploding Rocks dish out severe damage to any creature standing next to them when they explode–get away from them when they start to steam! Dark Order and Light Chaos creatures suffer only half-damage from Exploding Rocks and Death Spikes.

Dark Order and Light Chaos creatures are also not slowed down by the patches of Scorched Earth, unlike creatures of other realms. They regenerate magic energy one and a half times faster from Energy Crystals of their own alignment than other creatures. Dark Order Energy Crystals are green; Light Chaos Energy Crystals are red.

The trees, boulders, and rock outcrops in mountain terrain aren't directly hazardous, but the leafy tree branches can obscure Exploding Rocks, and boulders and rock outcrops can be confused with Exploding Rocks if you're not looking closely.

WRATH UNLEASHED

PRIMA'S OFFICIAL STRATEGY GUIDE

Plains

Aligned Realm(s):
Dark Order

Elemental Features: Acid Pit, Acid Vent, Spore Plant, Energy Crystal, Death Spikes
Neutral Features: Boulder, rock outcrop, tree

Don't be fooled by its serene appearance: Plains terrain is just as deadly as any other Battle Arena, and unless you're controlling a Dark Order creature, you should expect a knock-down, drag-out fight.

Falling in an Acid Pool or running over an Acid Vent when it sprays into the air does heavy damage to your creature. Spore Plants spray a deadly poison if a creature stands next to them for more than a few seconds, and Death Spikes are always looking to pop up under a careless warrior. Dark Order creatures suffer much less damage from these obstacles. They also regenerate combat magic energy twice as quickly as other creatures when standing near Energy Crystals.

Boulders, rock outcrops, and trees are generally harmless environmental obstacles. Use them for cover, but don't accidentally stand next to a Spore Plant!

Sea

Aligned Realm(s):
Light Order

Elemental Features: Undertow Pools, Water Vent, Solar Strikes, Energy Crystal, Death Spikes
Neutral Features: Boulder, rock outcrop, tree

Sea terrain is a beach for Light Order creatures, but creatures from other realms might not find it so relaxing. Undertow Pools slow down creatures from any realm other than Light Order.

Water Vents and Solar Strikes randomly erupt, doing tremendous damage to most creatures–but much less to Light Order creatures. Watch for patterns of energy that appear on the ground; these signal an imminent Solar Strike. Keep your eyes peeled for the patches of Death Spikes as well.

Light Order creatures regenerate combat magic energy twice as quickly when standing next to Energy Crystals than do other creatures.

Boulders, rock outcrops, and trees make for decent cover in sea terrain, but be careful that they don't block your magic and melee attacks.

Swamp

Aligned Realm(s):
Dark Order,
Light Order

Elemental Features: Mud Pit, Mud Vent, Energy Crystal, Death Spikes
Neutral Features: Rock outcrop, tree, corrupted boulder

This fetid terrain is pocked with murky pools of stagnant water, Mud Pits that slow the movement of Dark Chaos and Light Chaos creatures, Death Spikes that pop out of the ground, and Mud Vents that shoot out toxic blasts at regular intervals. Dark Order and Light Order creatures suffer only half damage from the elemental hazards of swamps. They also regenerate magic energy one and a half times faster than other creatures when they stand next to Energy Crystals of their own alignment–blue Energy Crystals are for Light Order creatures and green Energy Crystals are for Dark Order creatures.

Neutral environmental obstacles include rock outcrops, trees, and corrupted boulders. As on every other terrain, these can be used as cover or to limit an enemy's movement if you can maneuver them into the obstacles.

BATTLE MODE & ARMY BUILDER

BATTLE MODE

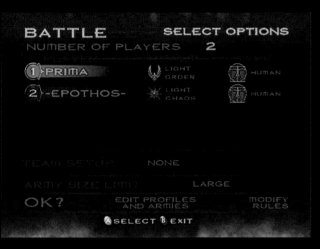

Think of Battle mode as a more versatile and open-ended version of Campaign mode. As in Campaign mode, the goal is to duel to victory in a World Map war by fulfilling preset conditions for victory. Unlike Campaign mode, however, you have near-total control over which Overlord you use, how many enemy or allied armies appear on the World Map with you, the creatures in your army, and the World Map on which you play. It's the ultimate *Wrath Unleashed* multiplayer experience!

To start a Battle game, choose "War Games" from the Main Menu, and then choose "Battle" from the War Games menu. This takes you to the Battle mode menu, shown in the screenshot above.

Players

Your first task when setting up a Battle game is choosing the number of players and the profiles and realms for each player, as well as the types of players they are.

NUMBER OF PLAYERS

You may choose to have two, three, or four players in the Battle game. Keep in mind that you can add AI (computer-controlled) players to the mix. If you have only two human players but want to play a four-player game, you can round out the game with two AI players.

Note

The number of players you choose determines which World Maps are available (see "World Map Menu," below). For instance, if you choose to play a three-player game, only three-player World Maps appear on the World Map menu. For more information on World Maps in Battle games, flip back a few pages to the "World Maps" section of this guide.

PROFILES

Next, choose a profile for each player by highlighting the name of the default profile (Aenna, Epothos, Durlock, or Helamis), selecting it, and then choosing a saved profile from the list that appears.

Note

If you choose to keep the default profile, your battle record won't be saved during the Battle game. That means you won't get credit for arena battles, which unlock hidden game features (see "Game Secrets" at the end of this guide for more information).

REALM

If you'd like your army to be aligned with a particular realm, change the value in the Realm field by highlighting and selecting it.

wrath
unleashed
chapter 7

battle mode &
army builder
♦ arena combat
♦ arenas

Note

The terrain that appears on the World Maps changes depending on which realm alignments the players choose, so don't bother selecting a realm that you think is going to give you a terrain advantage. No two players can have the same realm alignment.

Note

If you have allies in your Battle game, the conditions for victory can be achieved cooperatively. For instance, if you need to occupy seven Temple points, you can win if you occupy four and your partner occupies three. You can also cast friendly magic (Teleport, Heal, etc.) on your ally's creatures.

TYPE

Finally, choose what type of player each competitor is: Human, Easy AI, Normal AI, or Hard AI.

Team Setup

Team Setup only applies to three- and four-player Battle games. By default, all players are out for themselves. You can change the Team Setup value by highlighting it and selecting it. The arrangement of the player icons represents the team setup for the game, as shown in the following tables:

THREE-PLAYER TEAM SETUP

Icons	Team Setup
1, 2, 3	All three players are out for themselves (default).
1, 2 vs. 3	Players 1 and 2 are allied against Player 3.
1, 3 vs. 2	Players 1 and 3 are allied against Player 2.
1 vs. 2, 3	Players 2 and 3 are allied against Player 1.

FOUR-PLAYER TEAM SETUP

Icons	Team Setup
1, 2, 3, 4	All four players are out for themselves (default).
1, 2 vs. 3, 4	Players 1 and 2 are allied vs. Players 3 and 4.
1, 3 vs. 2, 4	Players 1 and 3 are allied vs. Players 2 and 4.
1, 4 vs. 2, 3	Players 1 and 4 are allied vs. Players 2 and 3.

Army Size Limit

The Army Size Limit option determines how large each player's army can be (how's that for obvious?). Battle games with larger armies generally take longer to complete. For more information on army sizes, skip down to "Army Builder," below.

Edit Profiles and Armies

Choose "Edit Profiles and Armies" if you want to change a player's profile or the army associated with it. Unless you change it, each profile's army is the default army of the size chosen in the Army Size Limit option. To create custom armies, check out "Army Builder," below.

Modify Rules

Battle mode Modify Rules menu

Six rules can be customized in Battle mode. Choose "Modify Rules" from the Battle menu to reach the Modify Rules menu and change the following options:

TURN LIMIT

This sets the maximum number of turns for the Battle game. If no player has won the game by the end of the turn limit, the game is a draw. You can turn the limit off or set it to 20, 25, 30, 35, or 40 turns.

TURN TIMER

If you use the Turn Timer option, each player has a time limit each turn to decide on a move. If the player doesn't make a decision within the time limit, the turn is automatically passed. You can turn the timer off or set it to 30, 60, 90, or 120 seconds.

BATTLE MODE &
ARMY BUILDER

ARENA TIMER

The Arena Timer option sets a time limit for each arena combat fight. If neither creature is victorious at the end of the time limit, magic bolts rain down from the sky until one or both creatures are killed. You can turn the timer off or set it to 60, 90, or 120 seconds.

MANA

The rate of Mana accumulation per turn is determined by the Mana option. By default, it is set to Normal, but you can also change it to Meager (less Mana than usual) or Mega (more Mana that usual).

ARENA COMBAT

The Arena Combat option is helpful in games with one or more AI players. If it's set to All Battles, the human players fight in all their arena battles and have to watch all AI battles. If you choose "Human Only," you fight in each battle that has a human player in it but skip any AI-vs.-AI scraps. You can also choose "No Battles" to skip all arena battles.

Note

Skipped arena battles are resolved automatically, based on the rank of the creatures involved and their current health. This levels the playing field if any of the human players are not experienced with the arena combat portion of *Wrath Unleashed*.

OVERLORD KILLED

This option determines what happens if a player's Overlord is killed in a Battle game. By default, it is set to Player Out, which means that the player loses the game and all of that player's creatures disappear from the World Map. You can switch it to Player In, where the player's army is allowed to continue fighting even after their Overlord is killed.

World Map Menu

When you have set all the Battle menu options, highlight and select "OK" in the bottom left corner of the screen to proceed to the World Map menu.

The World Map menu displays a list of all World Maps available for the type of Battle game you've set up. Highlight the name of a World Map to see a preview of it on the left side of the screen. A list of information about the World Map, including its relative difficulty, its Temple point total, and its win conditions appears under the preview.

Once you see a World Map you like, select it and choose "Start Game" to begin the Battle game or "Briefing" to see a short paragraph of information about the World Map.

Note

For more detailed information and strategies for each World Map, turn back to the "World Maps" section of this guide.

ARMY BUILDER

If you don't want to use the default army for your profile, take a look at the Army Builder feature in *Wrath Unleashed*, which allows you to set up custom armies. To reach the Army Builder menu, choose "War Games" from the Main Menu and "Army Builder" from the War Games menu.

First, you have to define the realm and size of the army. The realm determines the types of creatures you can choose from, and the army size (Large, Medium, or Small) determines how many creatures you can have in the army. Once you've set those options, select "Army Name" to name the army.

Edit Army Layout

Now choose the creatures that will make up your army. Select "Edit Army Layout" to go to the Edit Layout menu.

PRIMA'S OFFICIAL STRATEGY GUIDE

*wrath
unleashed
chapter 7*

**battle mode &
army builder**
♦ *arena combat*
♦ *arenas*

Your choice of creatures is limited by two factors. First, you can only have a certain number of each rank of creature in your army (see the "Rank Limits" table, below). Rank limits are indicated by the number of empty boxes to the right of the creature portraits on the left side of the screen.

> ## Note
> You can–and must–have one Overlord per army, regardless of the size of the army. Your army isn't complete until you've added an Overlord to it.

RANK LIMITS

Rank	Max. # Per Army
Overlord	1 (mandatory)
Champions	3
Warriors	5
Sentinels	7

Also, you have a finite number of creature points to use to construct your army. The number of creature points you have depends on the size of the army you've chosen to create.

CREATURE POINTS BY ARMY SIZE

Army Size	Creature Points
Large	40 points
Medium	30 points
Small	20 points

This means that even if you have empty rank slots, you might not be able to add another creature of that rank to your army if you have run out of creature points. For example, let's say that you're creating a small Light Order army, and you've chosen a Demigod Overlord (8 points) and two Frost Dragons (5 points apiece). You still have a Champion slot remaining, but you can't add another Frost Dragon, because you only have 2 creature points remaining (20 initial points minus 8 for the Overlord and 10 for the two Frost Dragons, equals 2).

CREATURE POINT COSTS

Light Order Creature	Light Chaos Creature	Dark Order Creature	Dark Chaos Creature	Rank	Creature Point Cost
Centaur	Centaur	Centabra	Centabra	Sentinel	
Unicorn	Unicorn	Dark Unicorn	Dark Unicorn	Sentinel	
Giantess	Giantess	Spirit Armor	Spirit Armor	Warrior	
Genie	Genie	Djinn	Djinn	Warrior	
Water Elemental	Fire Elemental	Earth Elemental	Wind Elemental	N/A	
Ogre Mage	Fire Giant	Iron Golem	Cyclops	Champion	
Frost Dragon	Blaze Dragon	Arch Demon	Chaos Demon	Champion	
Juggernaut Adept	Juggernaut Adept	Nightmare Adept	Nightmare Adept	Champion	
Demigod (Aenna)	Demigod (Epothos)	Demigod (Durlock)	Demigod (Helamis)	Demigod	
God (Aenna)	God (Epothos)	God (Durlock)	God (Helamis)	God	

CREATING ARMIES

There's no absolute, set-in-stone "right" way to create an army. But there are plenty of wrong ways, and here are six to avoid:

Don't confuse quantity with quality.
Five Centaurs have a combined health total greater than that of one Frost Dragon, but that doesn't necessarily mean that they're worth more. You can Resurrect a fallen Frost Dragon with one spell. What are the odds that you'll be able to move all five Centaurs into attack position as easily as one Frost Dragon?

Don't confuse quality with quantity.
A single Frost Dragon might be able to whup just about any enemy creature in single combat, but how well does it fare after three or four fights? And how are you going to occupy Mana Wats, Temples, Citadels, and Nexus Points if you only have five hugely powerful creatures in your army?

Don't feel like you have to customize an army.
If you're new to *Wrath Unleashed*, just use the default armies until you get a feel for the individual creatures. Regardless of a creature's power, it's ultimately only as useful as its player is skilled.

Don't choose creatures you don't like.
Don't feel like you have to choose a variety of creatures just for variety's sake. If you really like using Centaurs and you can't control a Unicorn to save your live, don't add Unicorns to your army unless the World Map calls for a lot of teleporting creatures.

Don't forget about your Battle Record.
Check out your profile's Battle Record from time to time to see how you're actually doing in arena combat; the results might shock you. You might think that you're hot stuff with Fire Giants until you realize that you have a mere 35 percent win percentage with them!

Don't leave any creature points unspent.
Make sure that you've purchased as many creatures as your point and rank limits allow. It's not a big deal if you have a point or two left over because you prefer Ogre Mages to Frost Dragons, but don't leave the Edit Layout menu if you still have a dozen unspent points.

Once you've chosen your army's creatures, choose "OK" at the bottom of the screen to return to the Army Builder menu. Press "Exit" if you want to return to the Army Builder menu without keeping the changes you made to the army layout.

Loading and Saving Armies
At the bottom of the Army Builder menu are three options: Load Army, Save Army, and Undo Changes.

LOAD ARMY
If you want to modify an army that you created and saved previously, use this option to load it and then edit it as usual.

SAVE ARMY
Once your army looks the way you want it, don't forget to save it by selecting this option.

UNDO CHANGES
Select this option to return the army layout to its original state, undoing any changes made since you last saved it. If you haven't saved the army at all, this returns it to its original default state.

CAMPAIGN MODE

wrath unleashed chapter 8

campaign mode
- arena combat
- arenas

CAMPAIGN   SELECT MISSION

PLAYER   PROFILE

1 PRIMA   PRIMA

LIGHT ORDER

DARK ORDER

Ⓐ SELECT Ⓑ EXIT

Campaign mode is a series of missions (actually, four series of missions) that collectively develop the stories of the four Overlords: Aenna, Epothos, Durlock, and Helamis. Each has a specific goal that you must achieve to complete the mission. Check out the mission objectives before playing, because most require you to do something other than capture Temples.

Each realm has its own series of four missions, and the missions get increasingly difficult as you move right or down along the Campaign mode menu. That is, Light Order Mission 1 is easier than Light Order Mission 4, which is easier than Dark Chaos Mission 4. At the start of Campaign mode, Mission 1 is unlocked for each realm. To unlock additional missions, complete the unlocked missions in sequence.

Tip

Start with Light Order Mission 1, complete all four Light Order missions, then move on to Light Chaos Mission 1. Complete the Light Chaos missions in order, then the Dark Order missions, and finally the Dark Chaos missions.

Unlocking Hidden Items

Completing Campaign mode missions unlocks hidden game features and items. For more information on unlocking items, turn to the "Game Secrets" section at the end of this guide.

UNLOCKING FEATURES IN CAMPAIGN MODE

Mission	Unlocked Feature
Mission 1 in each realm	Two Bonus Gallery images for that realm.
Mission 3 in each realm	Two more Bonus Gallery images for that realm
Mission 4 in each realm	That realm's God Overlord
Light Order Mission 2	Red 5 World Map
Light Chaos Mission 2	Frenzy World Map
Dark Chaos Mission 2	Grandmaster World Map
All 16 missions	Death Star World Map; Realm Master medal
All Light Order missions	Light Order Campaign medal
All Light Chaos missions	Light Chaos Campaign medal
All Dark Order missions	Dark Order Campaign medal
All Dark Chaos missions	Dark Chaos Campaign medal

CAMPAIGN MODE

THE STRUGGLE FOR GAIA'S THRONE, PART ONE

Regardless of which campaign you choose to begin, you see the following opening sequence:

Helana appears before Epothos at the Throne of Gaia and tries to seduce him and form an alliance. Epothos refuses, saying that as long as he has the power to fight, he'll never make an alliance with her.

Aenna offers her alliance to Epothos to defeat Helana and her dark brother, Durlock. Epothos tells her that he enjoys the peace between them, but he does not need her assistance. As Aenna vanishes, Epothos says that even she doesn't suspect his true power.

Epothos senses Durlock's presence but leaves the vicinity of the Throne of Gaia after finding himself unable to confront the Dark Order Demigod. Durlock appears and delivers a soliloquy in which he promises to conquer his rival Demigods and ascend to the Throne of Gaia himself.

LIGHT ORDER CAMPAIGN

The Light Order Campaign puts you in charge of Aenna's Light Order army. It is the easiest of the four campaigns, and it's the perfect place for a novice player to begin.

Mission 1: Dark Covenant

To complete Dark Covenant, occupy the Ambrosia Bloom in the center of the World Map.

LO MISSION 1 MAP KEY

🛕	Citadel	👑	Temple
🔘	Gate	◎	Sentinel
🛕	Magic Amplifier	◎	Warrior
⚜	Mana Wat	⊗	Champion
🏛	Nexus Point	🎛	Overlord

PRIMA'S OFFICIAL STRATEGY GUIDE

*wrath
unleashed
chapter 8*

*campaign
mode*

◆ *arena combat*
◆ *arenas*

THE MISSION

Durlock promises to help Aenna find her Crown of Ages, but can he be trusted?

Aenna's most prized possession, the Crown of Ages, has been stolen. Aenna suspects that its disappearance might be part of a larger plot to control the Throne of Gaia, but she can't act without evidence. Durlock offers to assist Aenna, provided that she's willing to fetch him some ambrosia, the drink of the gods, to refresh him before he exerts himself on her behalf.

THE BATTLEFIELD

All your most powerful creatures start out far from the Ambrosia Bloom.

You have one and only one goal: to occupy the Ambrosia Bloom in the center of the spiraling World Map. Unfortunately, your most powerful creatures (three Ogre Mages) start the mission at the farthest point possible from the Ambrosia Bloom. Several powerful enemy creatures stand between them and the Ambrosia Bloom, and there's a 30-turn limit for the mission, so you have your work cut out for you.

USE THE GATES

The two pairs of Gates let you cover a lot of ground quickly.

There are two pairs of Gates (red and blue) on the World Map. The first red Gate is near your Ogre Mages, and the second one is approximately a third of the way around the spiraling World Map. The first blue Gate is next to the second red Gate, and the second blue Gate is two-thirds of the way to the center of the World Map and the Ambrosia Bloom found there. Send your Ogre Mages through these Gates to cover ground quickly.

UNICORN BEACHHEAD

Send your teleporting Unicorns straight to the Ambrosia Bloom to take out the Dark Unicorns.

You also have two Unicorns near your Ogre Mages that can teleport across the narrow gap separating them from the Ambrosia Bloom area. Although they're probably not strong enough to take out the Cyclops that guards the Ambrosia Bloom, they can take out some or all of the nearby Dark Unicorns and establish a beachhead for your Ogre Mages.

Tip

Whenever possible, fight on the glacier terrain, which is aligned with your army and your Dark Chaos adversary, instead of the dead terrain that gives your enemy a huge advantage in combat. Lure the enemy Dark Unicorns on to the glacier terrain rather than pursuing them onto the dead terrain.

CAMPAIGN MODE

MANA WATS

Use your other three Unicorns to capture Mana Wats and Temples.

You have three more Unicorns on the side of the World Map opposite the Ogre Mages' starting positions. Near here are two Temples and three Mana Wats, most guarded by weak creatures. Use your Unicorns to occupy the Temples and Mana Wats to boost your Mana accumulation rate.

A Nightmare Adept guards one of the Temples. The only way to attack the Nightmare Adept is with Unicorns, because it is on the other side of a small gap that must be teleported across.

Tip

Ignore the Nightmare Adept and take the punishment of its spells unless you're a good enough arena fighter to take out the much more powerful Nightmare Adept with your Unicorns. Remember, the Nightmare Adept can only cast spells when it has the Mana to do it, so seizing the Mana Wats and Temples can be an offensive maneuver in and of itself.

OVERLORD SUPPORT

Your Overlord can't move, but she can cast spells from a distance.

Your Overlord is stuck on a Temple on a tiny island that floats on the outskirts of the World Map. She can't cast Teleport on herself to move into the field of battle, because the Temple prevents magic from being cast on that tile.

However, she can use her Wrath and Summon Elemental spells to destroy the nearby Spirit Armors and clear a path for the Ogre Mages to march down on their way to the Ambrosia Bloom. She can also Heal the Ogre Mages when they get within range.

Tip

Keep your Ogre Mages' health as high as possible for their assault on the Ambrosia Bloom. Use your Overlord and Unicorns to take out the enemies in their path so they don't have to scrap with anyone but the Cyclops guarding the Ambrosia Bloom.

Mission 2: Demon Hunt

Find and defeat the hidden Chaos Demon to complete the mission.

PRIMA'S OFFICIAL STRATEGY GUIDE

*wrath
unleashed
chapter 8*

*campaign
mode*
♦ *arena combat*
♦ *arenas*

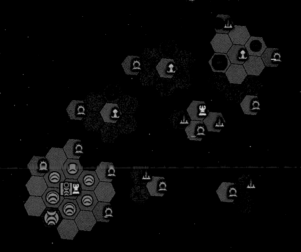

LO MISSION 2 MAP KEY

	Citadel		Temple
	Gate		Sentinel
	Magic Amplifier		Warrior
	Mana Wat		Champion
	Nexus Point		Overlord

THE MISSION

Helamis stole the Crown of Ages. Time to make her pay!

With Durlock's assistance, Aenna discovers that Helamis stole the Crown of Ages. Helamis retreats to a chaotic region of ethereal space in the hopes of shaking Aenna, but the Light Order Demigod manages to track her to a fragmented World Map held together with a series of Gates. Aenna's goal (and yours) is to find Helamis' hidden Chaos Demon and defeat it to recover the Crown of Ages.

THE GATES

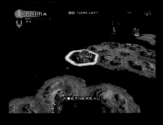
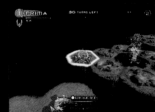

Red, blue, and yellow Gates are paired; each leads to an island with a Nexus Point.

Demon Hunt has four colors of Gates. All your forces start on one island that has one Gate of each color. Use the red, blue, and yellow Gates to reach the three islands with Nexus Points.

Note
One of the green Gates also leads to an island with a Nexus Point, but it's easier to reach that Nexus Point via the yellow Gate, so use that one if possible.

The five green Gates are best used to reach Mana Wats and Temples.

The five green Gates link five of the seven islands. Use the green Gates to cover a lot of ground in a hurry. Occupy Temples and Mana Wats to boost your Mana production. Send your weaker Sentinel creatures (Unicorns and Centaurs) out to occupy vacant Mana Wats and Temples while your Frost Dragon, Overlord, and Genies take possession of the Nexus Points.

NEXUS POINTS

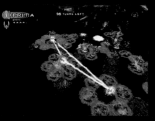

Control all three Nexus Points to activate them and reveal the rest of the World Map.

Your first goal should be to occupy the three Nexus Points simultaneously, because it's impossible to complete this mission until you trigger all three of them. A Centabra guards one, another has a Djinn near it, and the third is protected by a Nightmare Adept and two Dark Unicorns.

> # Tip
> If possible, use your Genies against the Centabra, your Frost Dragon against the Djinn, and your Overlord against the Nightmare Adept. Nothing lays the groundwork for victory better than coming into a fight with a power advantage.

CHAOS DEMON

The Chaos Demon is revealed once the Nexus Points are activated.

When you occupy all three Nexus Points simultaneously, land bridges appear and link all of the islands together into one land mass. The Chaos Demon is revealed on a Temple near what was an island with two Mana Wats and a Temple. Two additional Centabras are also revealed near the Chaos Demon.

When you defeat the Chaos Demon, the mission is complete!

There's nothing fancy about the last part of the mission–just send your forces swarming toward the Chaos Demon and throw everything you've got at it. As long as your Overlord survives and the Chaos Demon is defeated, you win!

> # Tip
> Use your Overlord against the Chaos Demon only as a last resort. Your Frost Dragon can really soften it up, and your Genies aren't too bad either. Your Unicorns and Centaurs probably wind up as a light snack for the Chaos Demon, but even they can inflict a bit of damage in a fight. Remember, defeating the Chaos Demon is the last thing you have to do. Once it's dead, it doesn't matter if your Overlord is your only remaining creature.

Mission 3: Vengeance

Capture seven Temple points or defeat Helamis in arena combat to win.

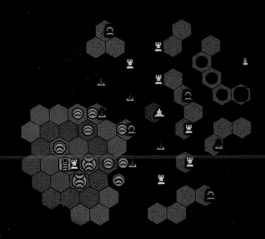

campaign mode
- *arena combat*
- *arenas*

LO MISSION 3 MAP KEY

Citadel		Temple	
Gate		Sentinel	
Magic Amplifier		Warrior	
Mana Wat		Champion	
Nexus Point		Overlord	

THE MISSION

Aenna must confront and defeat Helamis.

After defeating Helamis' Chaos Demon in the last mission, Aenna chases the Dark Chaos Overlord back to her own realm. There, Aenna fights Helamis on her own turf, both to punish Helamis for her thieving ways and to ensure that she doesn't represent a future threat to Aenna.

MAGIC AMPLIFIER

The Magic Amplifier in the center of the map is of immense strategic importance.

Your first move should be to seize the Magic Amplifier in the center of the map with your nearby Unicorn. From this Magic Amplifier, you can attack just about every one of Helamis' creatures with offensive spells and cast restorative magic on your own creatures as you move them forward.

Tip

Having control of the Magic Amplifier also lets you Teleport creatures near Temples and into combat with Helamis' troops.

MOVE FROM MANA WAT TO TEMPLE

All the Temples are on Helamis' side of the World Map.

Almost all of the Temples are just past the middle of the World Map, on Helamis' side, but all of the Mana Wats are on your side. Move your creatures onto the Mana Wats and, from there, onto the Temples. This ensures a steady flow of Mana for use by the creature on the Magic Amplifier.

Note

One of the really nice things about this World Map is that all six of the Temples are on terrain that favors your creatures in combat (glacier, swamp, and sea). Only two Temples are on glacier terrain, which also favors Helamis' troops.

CAMPAIGN MODE

GATES

All four Gates are red, and each is no more than two tiles away from a Temple.

Don't overlook the four red Gates in the center of the World Map. Entering any of them allows you to transport to any of the other three Gates, and none is more than two tiles away from a Temple.

Tip

Use your teleporting Unicorns to reach unoccupied Temples quickly by crossing the gaps in the World Map. When you want to take a Temple that Helamis has occupied, however, send larger creatures through the Gates to assault the Temple. When you take control of the Temple, you'll have a defender with some health energy left.

Mission 4: Aenna's Ascendance

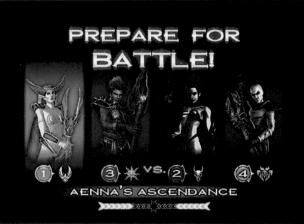

Partner with Epothos to seize six Temple points or defeat Helamis and Durlock.

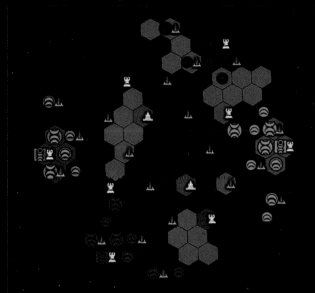

LO MISSION 4 MAP KEY

🏰	Citadel	♛	Temple
⚱	Gate	◎	Sentinel
🏛	Magic Amplifier	◉	Warrior
⚗	Mana Wat	⊗	Champion
♟	Nexus Point	▣	Overlord

THE MISSION

Defeating Helamis and Durlock gives Aenna possession of the Throne of Gaia.

The final battle of the Light Order Campaign takes place on Armageddon Island, where Aenna has enlisted the aid of Epothos to take on the combined forces of Helamis and Durlock. The first team of allies to seize six Temple points between the two of them or to defeat both rival Overlords wins the mission.

123

UNOCCUPIED TEMPLES

Each of the four unoccupied temples is between two armies.

At the start of the game, the World Map has four unoccupied Temples and four Temples occupied by an Overlord. First, seize the Temple between your army and Helamis' army. Next, go after the Temple between your army and Epothos' army. With luck, this encourages the AI-controlled Epothos to seize the Temple between its army and Durlock's.

*wrath
unleashed
chapter 8*

*campaign
mode*
♦ *arena combat*
♦ *arenas*

MAGIC AMPLIFIERS

Gain control of at least one Magic Amplifier quickly.

There are two Magic Amplifiers on the World Map, one near your army and Epothos' army, and one near Helamis and Durlock's armies. After seizing any unoccupied Temples, make a move for either Magic Amplifier (or both, if you can pull it off). This extends the range of your spell casting and can turn the tide of battle decisively in your favor.

Note

From the Magic Amplifier, you can Teleport creatures onto Mana Wats or the other Magic Amplifier. You can also cast Summon Elemental on rivals occupying the other Magic Amplifier or the Mana Wats. If you control both Magic Amplifiers, your creatures can Heal each other and stand a much better chance of holding the structures.

MANA WATS

There are Mana Wats aplenty; quickly occupy them with your weaker creatures.

The 20 Mana Wats on the World Map aren't as high a priority as the Temples or the Magic Amplifiers, but move to take as many of them as possible after you've moved onto all the unoccupied Temples and Magic Amplifiers. Possessing these Mana Wats increases the versatility of your creatures on the Magic Amplifiers, letting them cut loose with more powerful spells more often.

Tip

Use Sentinels to occupy the Mana Wats. Not only can you take advantage of their innate barrier ability to slow the advance of enemy creatures, but you also free up your more powerful creatures to occupy structures of much greater importance, such as the Temples and Magic Amplifiers.

LIGHT CHAOS CAMPAIGN

The Light Chaos Campaign follows the story of the Light Chaos Demigod, Epothos. While a bit more challenging than the Light Order Campaign, it's still easier than either the Dark Order or Dark Chaos Campaigns. If you get stuck on some of the Light Chaos Campaign's later missions, try some of the early Dark Order Campaign missions.

Mission 1: Anguish

CAMPAIGN MODE

Epothos must defeat the invading Aenna by besting her in combat or capturing seven Temple points.

not in it, she demands justice for her fallen subjects. Capture seven Temple points before Aenna does, or defeat her in combat, to win the mission.

ISLAND TEMPLES

First things first: Grab the two Temples on the floating islands in the middle of the World Map.

Your first moves should be to take the two Temples on the four-tile islands floating in the middle of the World Map. Use your teleporting Unicorns to reach them quickly and occupy them before Aenna does.

> ## Tip
> If you want to win this mission without having to assault Aenna directly (and you do–she's a tough customer), you need to take all five Temples in the middle of the World Map.

OTHER TEMPLES

Teleporting Unicorns can reach Temples on the other side of small gaps.

For the three remaining Temples in the middle of the World Map, use a teleporting Unicorn to cross the narrow gap between your starting position and the Temple on the unfavorable glacier terrain.

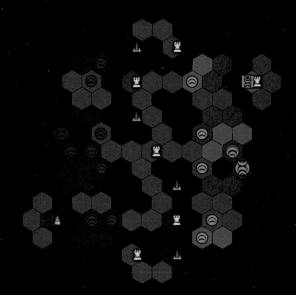

LC MISSION 1 MAP KEY

Citadel		Temple	
Gate		Sentinel	
Magic Amplifier		Warrior	
Mana Wat		Champion	
Nexus Point		Overlord	

THE MISSION

Aenna has been played for a fool, but Epothos has to stop her if he wants her to calm down.

Aenna invades Epothos' realm as retribution for an attack on her lands, for which she believes Epothos is responsible. Though her heart is clearly

*wrath
unleashed
chapter 8*

*campaign
mode*
♦ *arena combat*
♦ *arenas*

Note

This one can be tricky to hold, but if Aenna decides to try to take it back, that frees you up to go for the other Temples.

The two other Temples are easy to reach–they're three tiles ahead of your army in straight lines. One of them is on favorable mountain terrain; save this one for last, as it will be easier to take back from Aenna if she captures it. Instead, dedicate your efforts to conquering the Temple in the dead center of the World Map.

ISOLATED OVERLORD

Your Overlord is isolated on a small island far from combat, and it's not really worth moving him from it.

Both Aenna and Epothos are isolated on small islands at the very edges of the World Map; Epothos occupies a Citadel, and Aenna holds a Temple. You can move Epothos off the Citadel, Teleport him onto the mainland, then move a Unicorn across the gap and onto the Citadel to re-occupy it, but this is usually a waste of three moves. Your forces are powerful enough to take on Aenna's troops, provided that you have at least basic competency with arena combat.

Tip

Another reason not to move your Overlord into combat is that if he is killed, you lose the mission and must start over.

Mission 2: Ire

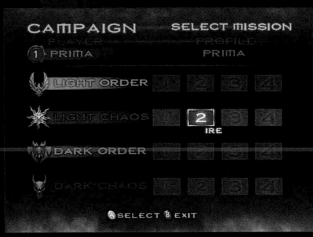

Defeat Helamis in combat or capture her Citadel to win.

LC MISSION 2 MAP KEY

🛡	Citadel	♖	Temple
⚱	Gate	◗	Sentinel
🏔	Magic Amplifier	◎	Warrior
⚠	Mana Wat	⊗	Champion
♟	Nexus Point	▣	Overlord

CAMPAIGN MODE

THE MISSION

Epothos decides to make Helamis pay for her deception.

Aenna tells Epothos why she attacked him: The sign of Epothos was left at the site of the carnage visited upon her realm. Epothos swears that he had nothing to do with the attack, and the two of them conclude that Helamis must be the guilty party. Epothos goes to Helamis' realm to punish her for her treachery. Helamis plays the innocent, trying to convince him that Aenna was the one trying to deceive him. When she sees that Epothos is having none of it, Helamis vows to defeat Epothos on the field of battle and show him the error of his ways.

HELAMIS' CITADEL

Helamis' Citadel is virtually impenetrable at the start of the mission.

At the start of the mission, Helamis is sitting in her Citadel on a single floating tile in the middle of the World Map. That makes it impossible for any creature except a Unicorn to attack her, and a Unicorn isn't going to get the job done, trust us.

CAPTURE THE MYTHIC FORGE

Capture the Mythic Forge to make your job a lot easier.

Instead, focus on occupying the Mythic Forge in the middle of the larger island in the center of the World Map. It's guarded by a Cyclops and three Dark Unicorns, but we have ways of dealing with them.

Move a Unicorn from a Mana Wat onto the Temple near the Mythic Forge.

First, move a Unicorn from a Mana Wat onto the Temple near the Mythic Forge. The Temple is on lava terrain, which gives your Unicorn a huge advantage in combat. This draws the Dark Unicorns into combat with the Unicorn. With the terrain advantage, you should be able to defeat them handily.

> ## Note
> Even if your Unicorn is injured in combat, it regenerates health between turns simply by sitting on the Temple tile.

HIDDEN TERRAIN REVEALED

Teleport a Blaze Dragon onto the Mythic Forge, defeat the Cyclops, and reveal the hidden terrain.

Once the Dark Unicorns have been dealt with, move your Overlord forward at least one tile. On the next turn, have your Overlord Teleport a Blaze Dragon directly into combat with the Cyclops on the Mythic Forge. The terrain is dead, which gives the Cyclops the advantage, but you should be able to do some serious damage even if you can't defeat it, and you have another Blaze Dragon that you can Teleport in on your next turn if you need to.

PRIMA'S OFFICIAL STRATEGY GUIDE

wrath
unleashed
chapter 8

campaign
mode
◆ arena combat
◆ arenas

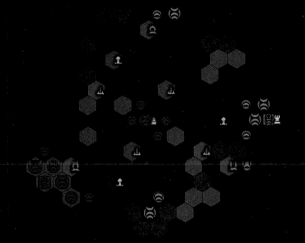

Caution

Do not Teleport your Overlord into combat with the Cyclops! Helamis is also within Teleport range of the Mythic Forge and can Teleport herself or her other Cyclops directly into battle on the Mythic Forge on her next turn. Once you've triggered the Mythic Forge, you don't need to keep occupying it. It's not a tragedy if you lose the Blaze Dragon that gained it. But if you lose your Overlord, you lose the mission.

Capturing the Mythic Forge causes a ring of lava terrain to appear around Helamis' Citadel, allowing you to move your more powerful forces directly into combat with her. At this point, all you need to do is fight effectively in arena combat, move your creatures down the field of battle, and defeat Helamis in combat to win. That might be easier said than done, but it doesn't require any fancy strategy other than the common sense you'd use in any other Battle or Campaign mission.

LC MISSION 3 MAP KEY

♨	Citadel	♛	Temple
♙	Gate	◉	Sentinel
♨	Magic Amplifier	◎	Warrior
♨	Mana Wat	◉	Champion
♟	Nexus Point	🔲	Overlord

Mission 3: Bonds of Darkness

Capture five Temple points to defeat Durlock.

THE MISSION

Durlock decides to ambush the weakened Epothos, in the hopes that he can defeat the fire lord and win Aenna's love.

After defeating Helamis, Epothos vows to cast her down into the abyss. Helamis begs him to reconsider the value of an alliance between the two of them, but Epothos turns a deaf ear to her pleas.

Still exhausted from his battle with Helamis, Epothos returns to his home realm only to find that Durlock has decided to take advantage of its owner's battle fatigue. Durlock vows to eradicate Epothos, claiming that Aenna deserves better than the Light Chaos Overlord.

CAMPAIGN MODE

NOT ENOUGH TEMPLES

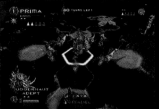

At the start of the game, there are only three Temple points.

One of the first things you'll notice at the start of the mission is that you need to capture five Temple points to win (or defeat Durlock), but only three Temple points are available: one Temple and one Citadel. What to do?

ACTIVATE NEXUS POINTS

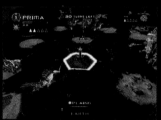

Occupy the three Nexus Points simultaneously to activate them and reveal new Temples.

Seizing control of the three Nexus Points on the World Map is your first priority. All are within two moves of your creatures' starting positions. One is on ethereal terrain, which makes it slightly harder to defend, but the other two are on lava and desert terrain, which give you a good terrain advantage and put Durlock's forces at a disadvantage.

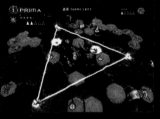

Occupying the Nexus Points reveals three more Temples.

Once you trigger all three Nexus Points, several new lava terrain tiles appear in the gaps of the World Map. Three of these tiles contain Temples. Now you can move your forces onto them and win the mission without having to defeat Durlock in combat!

Caution
Make sure that you're the one to activate the Nexus Points. If Durlock's forces do it, the terrain that the Temples appear on will be plains, which gives Durlock's creatures a huge advantage in combat.

GATES

The three blue Gates are all interconnected and give your opponents easy access to your army.

Finally, don't overlook the three blue Gates placed around the World Map, each on a sea terrain tile that gives no advantage to your forces or Durlock's.

These Gates are extremely useful for crossing the World Map to attack enemy creatures. Two are adjacent to Durlock's Sentinels; the third is directly in front of the bulk of your creatures.

Tip
Don't bother going after Durlock's creatures through the Gates. The Sentinels near them slow you down, and they don't offer much of a tactical advantage. You can fight the enemy creatures on the other side of them, but you have to fight on unfriendly terrain, which is never a smart idea. Instead, focus on capturing Nexus Points and Temples, and fight Durlock's creatures when they come to you.

Mission 4: Might of Epothos

Team up with Aenna to capture six Temple points between you, or defeat Helamis and Durlock in battle.

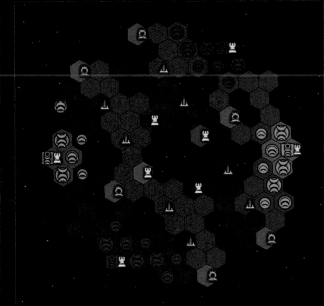

LC MISSION 4 MAP KEY

 Citadel		Temple
Gate		Sentinel
Magic Amplifier		Warrior
Mana Wat		Champion
Nexus Point		Overlord

THE MISSION

Epothos vows to defeat Helamis and Durlock once and for all for dominion over the Throne of Gaia.

With Aenna by his side, Epothos goes to confront Durlock for possession of the Throne of Gaia. Durlock has an ally in Helamis, however, and the final battle between Light and Dark begins!

TEMPLES

Capturing the four Temples in the center of the World Map is the easiest way to win.

At the start of the mission, there are eight Temples, four of them occupied by the four Overlords and four unoccupied in the center of the World Map.

Note

Each of the four unoccupied Temples is on terrain that favors the army farthest from it, so if you capture the Temple closest to you, you won't get a terrain advantage.

The closest Temple to Epothos is on a sea terrain tile, but you don't have to worry about Aenna trying to take it from you.

First, capture the Temple on the sea terrain tile. Not only is this one of the Temples closest to your

CAMPAIGN MODE

army, but you also don't have to worry about an enemy having a terrain advantage if they try to take it from you, because the sea terrain favors your ally, Aenna.

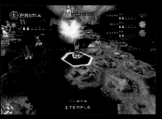

Move on to the Temple on the lava terrain, placing forces on Mana Wats as you do.

Next, press on and seize the Temple on the lava terrain near Helamis' army. Even if an enemy creature has occupied it, you have a big terrain advantage in combat that should turn the tide of battle in your favor.

Tip

While you're moving your troops, go from Mana Wat to Mana Wat. This ensures a steady flow of Mana, which can be used to Teleport powerful creatures to strategic positions, Heal injured defenders, or attack enemies with Wrath and Summon Elemental spells.

GATES

There are two types of Gates: red and blue.

Six Gates are scattered around the World Map, three red and three blue. These provide an excellent way to cross vast distances instantly. Use them to reinforce your ally's position if they're being attacked, capture an undefended Temple, or attack a weakened enemy.

Tip

Keep an eye on the Gates nearest the Temples that you and your ally have seized. They make convenient back doors for your adversaries to assault Temples that you aren't defending as well as you should.

DARK ORDER CAMPAIGN

The Dark Order Campaign revolves around the Demigod Durlock, and it is more challenging than either the Light Order or Light Chaos Campaigns. The skills you acquire in the earlier campaigns will serve you well in these challenging missions.

Mission 1: Deceit

Defeat Epothos or capture his Citadel to win.

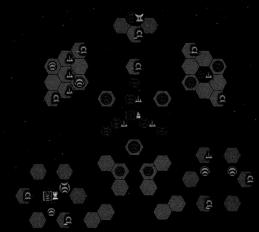

DO MISSION 1 MAP KEY

🛡	Citadel	🏆	Temple
🚪	Gate	🔵	Sentinel
🔱	Magic Amplifier	🔵	Warrior
⚠	Mana Wat	🔵	Champion
🗼	Nexus Point	🔳	Overlord

THE MISSION

Epothos is foolish enough to grant hospitality to Durlock. Teach him the error of his generosity.

Durlock arrives in Epothos' realm, and Epothos tells him to leave immediately. Durlock says that he is on a long journey and needs only to rest for a moment in Epothos' lands. Considering him too pathetic to strike down, Epothos allows Durlock access to his lands. As soon as Durlock is admitted, he turns on his host and attacks Epothos.

THE ALTAR

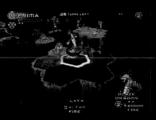

You must defeat the Blaze Dragon guarding the Altar if you want so much as a prayer of defeating Epothos.

Epothos is in the center of the World Map, his Citadel guarded by a half-dozen Fire Giants. A frontal attack with your limited forces is suicide. Instead, focus on capturing the Altar guarded by the Blaze Dragon on the six-tile island.

Tip

In this World Map, knowing where *not* to go is as important as knowing where to go. Avoid the diamond-shaped island with the two Genies and the Centaur–it's relatively easy to move around the World Map without setting foot on that island and getting into an unnecessary fight.

GATES

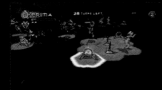

The four green Gates link the two diamond-shaped islands with the Altar and the main island.

Your first priority is to activate the Altar, and the best way to do that is to use the network of Gates on the World Map to reach it. The four

green Gates link the Altar island with the mainland and the two diamond-shaped islands.

Tip

Move your forces onto the Altar island via the green gate on the diamond-shaped island with the three Mana Wats and your Djinn and Centabra.

The red and blue Gates are paired and link the diamond-shaped islands to the mainland.

To move your forces from the swampy edges of the main island to the diamond-shaped islands, use the pairs of red and blue Gates. Each side of the World Map has one pair.

The pair of yellow Gates connects the corners of the main island farthest from Epothos' Citadel.

Finally, the pair of yellow Gates links the two swampy areas of the main island. Use these to quickly move from one side of the island to the other.

CONQUERING THE ALTAR

Send your Iron Golem or Demigod, or both, into battle against the Blaze Dragon that guards the Altar.

CAMPAIGN MODE

Your Iron Golem and Demigod are the best creatures to use against the Blaze Dragon that guards the Altar. Remember that the Altar is on lava terrain, which greatly favors the Blaze Dragon.

Use the blue Gate near your Demigod and Iron Golem to move them to the diamond-shaped island with the three Mana Wats, and from there, use the green Gate to reach the Altar.

Tip

It's very important to move carefully around the diamond-shaped island with the three Mana Wats. Stay to the outer edge of the island. If you come any closer to the center of the World Map, your forces are vulnerable to spells cast by Epothos in his Citadel.

IRON GOLEM REINFORCEMENTS

Three Iron Golems appear on newly revealed terrain once you capture the Altar.

Once you capture the Altar, three Iron Golems appear on new tiles that link the islands with the mainland, and three of Epothos' Fire Giants are instantly destroyed. This evens the odds considerably!

Tip

If you have plenty of turns left, see if you can lure the Fire Giants into attacking your Iron Golems on mountain terrain, which gives an advantage to both creatures, rather than scrapping on lava, which puts the odds squarely in the Fire Giants' favor.

Now that you're on more even footing with your adversary, it's just a matter of sending in every creature you've got to destroy Epothos and his fiery guardians.

Tip

Save Durlock for a last-ditch assault on Epothos. Make sure he's never closer than six tiles to Epothos (out of spell range), and keep sending creatures in to damage Epothos. Once you've hurt Epothos, send in Durlock to finish the job.

Mission 2: Ungodly Alliance

Capture seven Temple points or defeat both Helamis and Epothos in combat to win.

WRATH UNLEASHED
PRIMA'S OFFICIAL STRATEGY GUIDE

DO MISSION 2 MAP KEY

🔥	Citadel	♜	Temple
⛩	Gate	◉	Sentinel
🏛	Magic Amplifier	◎	Warrior
⚗	Mana Wat	✕	Champion
♟	Nexus Point	▣	Overlord

THE MISSION

It has to be seen to be believed–Helamis and Epothos actually working together.

Durlock retreats to his home realm after defeating Epothos in combat, only to find that Epothos and Helamis, Durlock's sister, have formed an unlikely alliance to destroy him.

OUTNUMBERED?

The two-on-one fight doesn't seem fair, until you realize you have more creatures than both foes combined!

At first glance, this seems like an extremely unfair mission, as you're put up against two foes with no allies to call your own. But a few aspects are in your favor.

Your first advantage is numerical. Each of your enemies has six creatures, including Overlords. You start off with 13, a slightly superior force.

You also have a tremendous terrain advantage. Two-thirds of the terrain is either plains, which greatly favors you, or swamp, which favors you and Aenna, who isn't part of this fight.

MAGIC AMPLIFIERS

You start out in possession of two Magic Amplifiers, a tremendous advantage.

Your third big advantage is the fact that you start out in possession of two Magic Amplifiers. You also begin the mission by occupying a Citadel, three Mana Wats, and three Temples, so you have a steady flow of Mana from the get-go.

Tip
From the start of the mission, one of Helamis' and one of Epothos' creatures are within range of offensive spells cast by your creatures on the Magic Amplifiers.

LET THEM COME TO YOU

Your general strategy should be to hold structures and attack from a distance with spells.

Use your many advantages to their fullest and wait for your foes to come to you. Occupy every unoccupied Mana Wat and Temple, then sit back and let your enemies send their creatures within range of your spell casters. If enemy creatures actually make it into combat with you, it will be on terrain that favors your creatures.

Caution

Do not, under any circumstances, take the fight to your enemies until they stop advancing on your Temples and Mana Wats. Only when your foes start passing turns with regularity should you invade their turf.

Mission 3: Envy

Reveal Epothos' hiding place and defeat him to win.

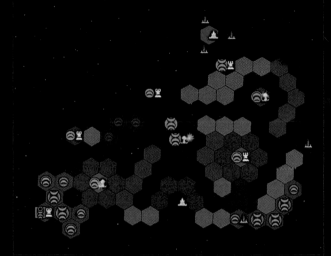

DO MISSION 3 MAP KEY

🏛	Citadel	♜	Temple
	Gate	◉	Sentinel
🏯	Magic Amplifier	◎	Warrior
⚱	Mana Wat	⊗	Champion
⚑	Nexus Point	🎰	Overlord

THE MISSION

Durlock thinks that beating up Epothos in front of his girlfriend will get her to leave him. He might be right....

After his humiliating defeat at the hands of Durlock, Epothos flees to Aenna's realm. Aenna hides him, but Durlock follows in hot pursuit. Aenna and Epothos' forces are poised to defeat Durlock before he can reveal Epothos' position and destroy him. Durlock vows to find the hidden Epothos and hand him a humiliating defeat in front of Aenna.

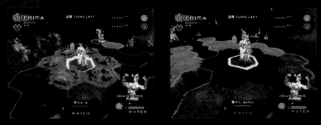

NEXUS POINTS

EPOTHOS REVEALED

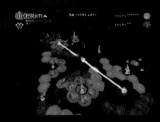

Two of the three Nexus Points are guarded by the relatively easy-to-defeat Giantesses.

Before you can defeat Epothos, you have to find him, and to do that, you have to occupy all three Nexus Points simultaneously. The two Nexus Points on the edges of the World Map are guarded by Giantesses, which are relatively easy to defeat with powerful creatures or with one or two smaller, faster creatures.

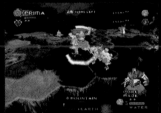

An Ogre Mage guards the Nexus Point in the center of the World Map, with a Juggernaut Adept nearby.

The third Nexus Point, in the center of the World Map, is occupied by an Ogre Mage backed up by a Juggernaut Adept. This is by far the most challenging Nexus Point to take—use larger, powerful creatures to take on and defeat the two defenders.

Tip

Although you're technically facing two enemies, only three of Epothos' Unicorns are on the World Map at the start of the mission, so it's pretty much a one-on-one fight between you and Aenna until you reveal Epothos with the Nexus Points. For that reason, you might want to delay revealing Epothos for a turn or two if it means you can dispose of a few more of Aenna's creatures.

The three Nexus Points, when activated, reveal Epothos' position.

When you occupy all three Nexus Points simultaneously, Epothos' hiding place is revealed—it's a small outcropping near the three lava terrain tiles that served as the starting location for his three Unicorns.

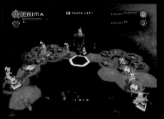

Several Centaurs and Dragons defend Epothos, and the terrain favors him and Aenna.

Once he's revealed, you still have to take him out. And that's not easy, because two Light Order Centaurs, a Light Order Unicorn, a Frost Dragon, and a Blaze Dragon also appear to help him. Also, the newly created terrain favors Aenna and, to a lesser extent, Epothos.

This is the World Map, after triggering the Nexus Points.

It's a tough fight. If you've taken out most of the Light Order and Light Chaos creatures that appeared at the start of the mission, you'll have an easier time of it.

wrath unleashed chapter 8

campaign mode
♦ *arena combat*
♦ *arenas*

CAMPAIGN MODE

chapter 1

chapter 2

chapter 3

chapter 4

chapter 5

chapter 6

chapter 7

chapter 8

chapter 9

chapter 10

Tip

Before you begin your assault on the newly created tiles, cast Transform Land on them to give yourself the advantage in combat against Epothos' defenders.

Mission 4: Durlock's Conquest

Defeat your three rivals or capture five Temple points to win the mission and complete the Dark Order Campaign path.

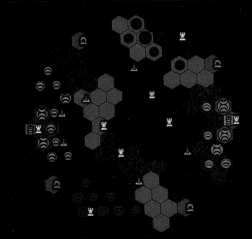

DOMISSION 4 MAP KEY

 Citadel   Temple

 Gate   Sentinel

Magic Amplifier   Warrior

 Mana Wat   Champion

 Nexus Point   Overlord

THE MISSION

Can Durlock overcome three rivals to conquer the Throne of Gaia?

While Durlock hunted Epothos, all four Overlords positioned their forces to conquer the Throne of Gaia. All alliances have been shattered–Epothos has lost the respect of Helamis and Aenna, who could never stand each other to begin with. Now everyone is as isolated as Durlock has always been, and in this final battle, it's every Overlord for himself or herself!

TEMPLES

Four unoccupied Temples are in the center of the World Map.

This World Map has eight Temples. Overlords occupy four; the other four, in the center of the World Map, are unoccupied.

Each Temple sits on terrain that is advantageous to two Overlords' armies, but the Temples that favor an army are on the farthest side of the World Map from that army.

Tip

If you're going to occupy Temples on unfavorable terrain, use Sentinel blockers between the Temple and the armies that find the terrain advantageous.

GATES

wrath
unleashed
chapter 8

campaign
mode
* *arena combat*
* *arenas*

Four red Gates, placed between rival armies, keep things interesting.

There are also four red Gates placed around the edges of the World Map. Entering any Gate allows you to instantly transport to any other Gate. You must defend your turf against enemies who might try using the Gates as a means of ambushing you.

You can also use the Gates, of course, and if an enemy is spread too thin, you might find it easier to attack an Overlord than it is to fight with that Overlord's creatures for possession of Temples.

Tip
The big advantage of taking out a rival Overlord isn't getting possession of the Temple that the Overlord defended, although that's also nice. Taking out rival Overlords destroys their entire army and opens up the playing field a bit more. Definitely consider sending larger creatures after Overlords whose troops have scattered in an attempt to capture Temples.

DARK CHAOS CAMPAIGN

The Dark Chaos Campaign, which tells the story of the Demigod Helamis, is the most challenging of the four realms' campaigns. If you're not an expert at arena combat, there's no point in even trying to complete these missions until you log some serious training hours.

Mission 1: Fury

Helamis must capture five Temple points to defeat Aenna.

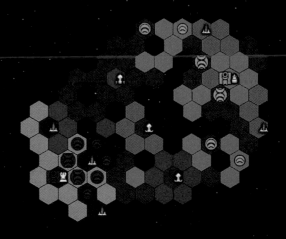

DC MISSION 1 MAP KEY

Citadel		Temple	
Gate		Sentinel	
Magic Amplifier		Warrior	
Mana Wat		Champion	
Nexus Point		Overlord	

THE MISSION

Helamis challenges Aenna to a catfight, with Epothos as the trophy.

Helamis invades Aenna's domain, vowing to defeat Aenna in combat and remove her as a rival for Epothos' affections. Aenna shrugs off Helamis' threats, claiming that her madness has blinded her to the fact that she has all but lost the battle already.

SEIZE THE NEXUS POINTS

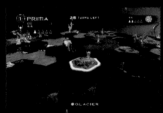

You can't win without occupying the Nexus Points and revealing the hidden Temples.

Your first goal in this mission should be to occupy all three Nexus Points simultaneously. Doing so reveals additional Temples and terrain. That new terrain favors the Overlord who activates the Nexus Points.

From your creatures' starting positions, you have a Centabra that can reach the center Nexus Point. A Chaos Demon can reach another, and a Cyclops can come within one tile of the third Nexus Point. Move these creatures toward the Nexus Points immediately.

Tip

If your opponent triggers the Nexus Points, you should probably just quit the game and restart the mission. It's not impossible to continue to victory, but it's extremely unlikely.

ACTIVATING THE NEXUS POINTS

Activating the Nexus Points fills in the huge gap in the World Map and reveals four Temples and two Magic Amplifiers.

When you activate the three Nexus Points, the largest gap in the World Map fills with terrain that gives your creatures an advantage in combat. This is especially significant because four Temples appear on the new terrain. Having those Temples resting on terrain that favors your creatures makes it easier to conquer and defend those Temples.

The Magic Amplifiers are also extremely valuable structures.

Two Magic Amplifiers also pop up on the new terrain. These are especially useful because you don't start the mission with a Nightmare Adept, making your Overlord the only spell caster in your army. Occupy the Magic Amplifiers immediately. Grab the one on your opponent's side of the World Map first, because it's the trickier one to occupy.

CONQUERING TEMPLES

You need five Temple points for victory.

To win this mission, you need to defeat Aenna in combat (hard) or conquer five Temple points (easier, especially if you activated the Nexus Points). At the start of the mission, there aren't enough Temple points for you to win by occupying structures, so you either have to trigger the Nexus Points or defeat Aenna.

The World Map, after you activate the Nexus Points.

We definitely recommend occupying the Nexus Points and revealing the four hidden Temples. Because the Temples rest on friendly terrain, you should have a fairly easy time holding them.

Mission 2: No Honor

wrath
unleashed
chapter 8

campaign
mode
◆ arena combat
◆ arenas

Occupy five Temple points or defeat Durlock in battle to win.

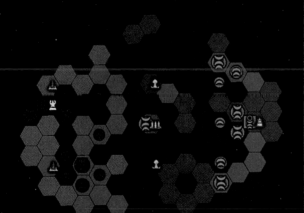

DC MISSION 2 MAP KEY

🏰	Citadel	👑	Temple
⬛	Gate	◉	Sentinel
🔺	Magic Amplifier	◉	Warrior
⚠	Mana Wat	◉	Champion
🔼	Nexus Point	📟	Overlord

THE MISSION

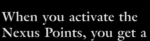

Durlock pulled Helamis away from Aenna before she could destroy Aenna, and Helamis isn't happy about it.

Concerned that Helamis will kill his beloved Aenna in her fury, Durlock transports his Dark Chaos sister to his realm. Helamis refuses to listen to Durlock's offer of an alliance, instead vowing to give him the punishment he deserves. For Helamis to escape, she must capture Durlock's Citadel or defeat him in combat.

SEIZE THE NEXUS POINTS

There are two Nexus Points to be captured. Be the one to hold them both.

The two Nexus Points in the center of the World Map are absolutely critical for victory. The first army to hold both at once causes several gaps to be filled in with terrain that favors them. Four Temples and two Mana Wats also appear.

Without activating the Nexus Points, your only hope for victory is to defeat Durlock in combat.

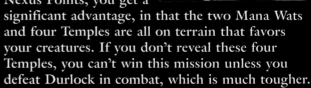

When you activate the Nexus Points, you get a significant advantage, in that the two Mana Wats and four Temples are all on terrain that favors your creatures. If you don't reveal these four Temples, you can't win this mission unless you defeat Durlock in combat, which is much tougher.

CIRCLE OF POWER

The Circle of Power stands in the center of the World Map.

In the dead center of the World Map, you find a structure called the Circle of Power, which is guarded by an Iron Golem.

Tip

One of the best ways to take out the Iron Golem is to Teleport your Overlord directly onto it. The Circle of Power is not protected against magical attack.

Capture the Circle of Power to get six more creatures and fill in the center gap with dead terrain.

If you capture the Circle of Power, you get an additional four Centabras and two Cyclopes. Also, the gap around the former site of the Circle of Power fills in with dead terrain, which is extremely favorable to your creatures.

The World Map after activating the Nexus Points and Circle of Power.

Tip

If you use your Overlord to capture the Circle of Power, remember that she is vulnerable after the battle. Fortunately, when the six creatures pop up around her, she's protected against walking creatures, since they can't get past the newly created Cyclopes and Centabras.

Mission 3: Scorned

To win, conquer seven Temple points with Durlock's assistance, or defeat Aenna and Epothos.

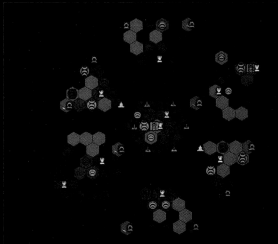

DC MISSION 3 MAP KEY

Citadel		Temple	
Gate		Sentinel	
Magic Amplifier		Warrior	
Mana Wat		Champion	
Nexus Point		Overlord	

WRATH UNLEASHED

PRIMA'S OFFICIAL STRATEGY GUIDE

THE MISSION

wrath
unleashed
chapter 8

campaign mode
◆ *arena combat*
◆ *arenas*

Is the element of surprise enough for Helamis and Durlock to defeat Epothos and Aenna?

Helamis joins forces with Durlock, to whom she taught a lesson after the last mission. The two of them ambush Aenna and Epothos and surround them. In this penultimate battle, Helamis and Durlock seek to utterly defeat their Light rivals by destroying their creatures and seizing their Temple points.

LEARN THE GATES

Yellow and green Gates link three adjacent islands.

Critical to winning this battle is an understanding of how to use the Gates to move around the six islands that surround the hexagonal seventh island in the center of the World Map, where Aenna and Epothos are trapped. The yellow and green Gates come in threes and are used to move around three adjacent islands along the edge of the World Map.

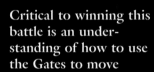

Red and blue Gates link two adjacent islands.

Red and blue Gates are paired, and each links one of the trapezoidal islands with the adjacent triangular island.

All six of the outlying islands hav███ ██ of creatures on them. Each is balanced quite fairly between Dark and Light forces except for the Overlords' islands, which have significantly more Dark forces on them. The terrain tends to favor your opponents, but knowing when and where to fight them can reduce this advantage.

CENTER ISLAND

Both of your rival Overlords can be found on the hexagonal center island.

Aenna and Epothos are both trapped on the center island with the two Temples and six Mana Wats. The island has no Gates, which makes it hard to step onto, but that also makes it tough for Aenna and Epothos to leave. The most dangerous thing about the island is its six Mana Wats, which pump Mana into their Overlords quickly.

MAGIC AMPLIFIERS

Use the Magic Amplifiers when attacking the center island.

If you can seize a Magic Amplifier or two, you're in an excellent position to attack the center island. F███ the Magic Amplifiers, you can Teleport ███ ██res into combat, Heal them after fights, and cast Summon Elemental and Bind on enemy creatures.

Tip

Anything you can do to stem your rivals' Mana flow helps protect you against their Overlords.

Mission 4: Dominion of Helamis

Helamis must defeat Durlock and the team of Aenna and Epothos, or capture five Temple points to win.

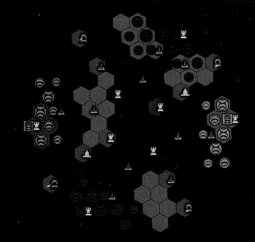

DC MISSION 4 MAP KEY

	Citadel		Temple
	Gate		Sentinel
	Magic Amplifier		Warrior
	Mana Wat		Champion
	Nexus Point		Overlord

THE MISSION

Helamis discards all allies in her mad quest for the Throne of Gaia.

After emerging victorious from her last mission, Helamis decides to press on and conquer the Throne of Gaia. However, when she arrives on the World Map, she finds that the other Overlords have maneuvered their forces into position as well. Helamis declares that she is sick of Durlock's scheming. She vows that Epothos will be hers, and that she will destroy Aenna once and for all. And so the final battle begins, pitting Helamis against Durlock and against the team of Aenna and Epothos.

Note

Helamis and Durlock each need to capture five Temple points to win, but Aenna and Epothos need to capture a combined seven Temple points to win.

CAPTURING TEMPLES

Each of the unoccupied Temples is on terrain that is advantageous to only one Overlord.

At the start of the game, there are eight Temples. Four are occupied by Overlords; four more, in the center of the World Map, are unoccupied. Each unoccupied Temple is on a type of terrain that greatly benefits only one Overlord. These Temples are, inconveniently, placed as far away from each Overlord's starting point as possible.

143

PRIMA'S OFFICIAL STRATEGY GUIDE

wrath
unleashed
chapter 8

campaign
mode
◆ arena combat
◆ arenas

Tip

In your scramble for Temple possession, don't forget the cardinal rule of these free-for-alls: Never interrupt a fight between your opponents! If Durlock, Aenna, and Epothos want to beat each other to a pulp, don't mess that up by attacking one of them!

GATES

The Gates are convenient back doors to each army's starting location.

Four yellow Gates are located at the edges of the World Map, each positioned between two armies' starting locations. You can use these Gates to teleport to the other side of the World Map and position yourself for seizing the Temple that's on the terrain that favors your army.

You can also use these Gates to attack your opponents directly, which is a great idea if the Overlord is undefended. Remember, defeating an Overlord removes that Overlord and his or her entire army from the game.

Caution

Don't forget that your enemies can use the Gates to ambush you just as easily as you can use the Gates to attack them. Make sure that you have Sentinel barriers in place to prevent a foe from transporting through a Gate and waltzing up to your Overlord.

MAGIC AMPLIFIERS

Magic Amplifiers can put those Mana Wats to good use.

Finally, two Magic Amplifiers are located on opposite sides of the World Map. Capturing and holding a Magic Amplifier is a great idea for two reasons: First, there are almost a dozen Mana

---

Wats on the World Map, and having a creature on a Magic Amplifier lets you make better use of them.

Second, you want to hold the Magic Amplifiers just to prevent your opponents from taking them and attacking you with spells. Better that you cast Summon Elemental against them than they do it to you!

END OF THE MISSION PATH

Regardless of which Overlord's campaign path you chose, the ending is virtually identical. The triumphant Overlord approaches the Throne of Gaia as the other three Overlords kneel.

All the defeated Overlords bow before the victor.

Ascending the throne, the Overlord rises into the air and is transformed into the God aspect in a flash of light, signifying unquestioned dominion over the Shattered Realms.

The victorious Overlord is transformed into a God.

You can now choose to use an Overlord's God aspect in Battle, Versus, and Team Fighter modes.

VERSUS AND TEAM FIGHTER MODES

VERSUS MODE

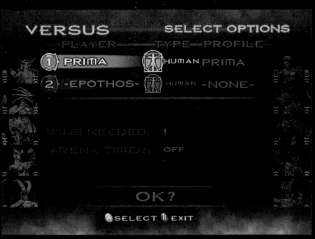

Versus mode uses the arena combat aspect of *Wrath Unleashed* and discards everything else, essentially transforming the game into a one-on-one fighting game. To access the Versus mode menu, choose "Versus" from the Main Menu.

Setting Up Versus Mode
Setting up a Versus mode game is easy: Choose the type of players involved (Human, Easy AI, Normal AI, Hard AI) and the profile associated with each player, if any.

WINS NEEDED
Then decide how many wins a player needs to be victorious in the Versus game. Set the value to 1, 2, 3, 4, 5, or Unlimited, in which the match doesn't end until one of the players quits out of it.

ARENA TIMER
Finally, decide if you want to use an arena timer in your Versus game. If the arena timer is set to 60, 90, or 120 seconds, that's how long the match lasts before it enters "Sudden Death" and bolts of magic rain down from the sky randomly until one or both characters are killed. If you don't want a time limit in your Versus game, set the Arena Timer option to Off.

Select Creatures

After setting up the Versus game, choose "OK?" from the bottom of the Versus mode menu to proceed to the Creature Select menu. Here, each player chooses a creature to use in the Versus mode game.

Tip
Some matchups might seem extremely unfair (Frost Dragon vs. Unicorn, for instance), but playing these types of Versus matches is a great way to hone your arena fighting skills. You might not be able to kill that Frost Dragon with your Unicorn, but if killing your Unicorn costs the Frost Dragon twice as much in health points, your skills will give you a tremendous advantage in Battle and Campaign mode games.

145

PRIMA'S OFFICIAL STRATEGY GUIDE

Select Arena

wrath
unleashed
chapter 9

**versus and
team fighter
modes**
♦ *team fighter*
♦ *versus mode*

After both players have chosen their creatures, highlight and select "OK?" from the bottom of the Creature Select menu to proceed to the Arena Select menu, where you–surprise!–select the arena in which you'll fight.

Tip
Remember that certain arenas favor certain realm alignments. See the "Arena Combat Training" section of this guide for more information on arena realm alignments.

Once the fight concludes, return to the Creature Select menu, where you can choose another pair of creatures and fight again, or press "Back" to return to the Versus menu.

Tip
Versus mode is a great way to rack up arena wins. The Defender medal is awarded when you reach 100 wins, and the Metal Age combat arena is unlocked at the same time.

TEAM FIGHTER

Team Fighter is an expanded version of *Wrath Unleashed*'s Versus mode. Like Versus mode, Team Fighter mode pits pairs of creatures against each other in arena combat. But a Versus match is a single duel between two creatures, and Team Fighter is a series of one-on-one arena fights between teams of creatures. Whichever team is wiped out first loses the Team Fighter match.

146

VERSUS AND TEAM FIGHTER MODES

Setting Up a Team Fighter Match

First choose a player type and profile for each player, just as you would in a Versus mode match (see "Setting Up Versus Mode," above). Then set the Team Size, Rank Limit, Arena Select, and Arena Timer options.

TEAM SIZE

Decide if you want large, small, or normal-sized teams. Choosing "Large" allows each player to choose more powerful team creatures and generally makes for a longer game. Small teams are made up of fewer, weaker creatures, and they tend to face off in shorter, simpler Team Fighter games.

RANK LIMIT

If Rank Limit is turned on, limits are placed on the number of each rank of creatures that you can have on your team, regardless of the number of creature points you have to work with. For instance, if you turn Rank Limit on, you can only have up to seven creatures of Sentinel rank, even if you have enough points to purchase an eighth. If Rank Limit is turned off, you can add as many creatures of any rank as you want, provided you have enough creature points to buy them.

ARENA SELECT

Between each round of combat in Team Fighter mode, a new arena is chosen for the next fight. How that arena is chosen depends on what Arena Select is set to:

Random: The next arena is selected randomly.
Winner Adv.: The next arena favors the winner of the last fight.
Neutral: Arenas that give neither player an advantage are automatically chosen.
Loser Adv.: The next arena favors the loser of the last fight.

ARENA TIMER

This option is similar to Arena Timer in several other game modes. Turning it on adds a 60-, 90-, or 120-second time limit to each round of combat. If neither creature emerges victorious at the end of the time limit, "Sudden Death" begins. Magical bolts rain down randomly until one or both creatures are dead.

Build Team

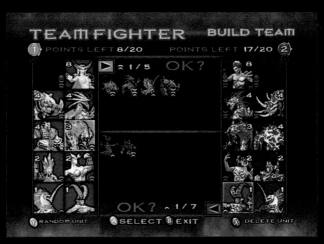

Once the Team Fighter game is set up, it's time to build each player's team. The Build Team menu is very similar to the Army Builder mode Edit Layout menu–you have a certain number of points (depending on what Team Size was set to) to add creatures to your team. If Rank Limit is turned on, you can only add a certain number of creatures of each rank to your team.

TEAM SIZE CREATURE POINT LIMITS

Team Size	Creature Point
Small	5
Medium	10
Large	20

RANK LIMITS

Rank	Max. # Per Army
Overlord	1
Champions	3
Warriors	5
Sentinels	7

Note

Unlike Battle mode's Army Builder, you don't have to put an Overlord on your team if you don't want to.

CREATURE POINT COSTS

Light Order Creature	Light Chaos Creature	Dark Order Creature	Dark Chaos Creature	Rank	Creature Point Cost
Centaur	Centaur	Centabra	Centabra	Sentinel	1
Unicorn	Unicorn	Dark Unicorn	Dark Unicorn	Sentinel	1
Giantess	Giantess	Spirit Armor	Spirit Armor	Warrior	2
Genie	Genie	Djinn	Djinn	Warrior	2
Water Elemental	Fire Elemental	Earth Elemental	Wind Elemental	Warrior	3
Ogre Mage	Fire Giant	Iron Golem	Cyclops	Champion	4
Frost Dragon	Blaze Dragon	Arch Demon	Chaos Demon	Champion	4
Juggernaut Adept	Juggernaut Adept	Nightmare Adept	Nightmare Adept	Champion	4
Demigod (Aenna)	Demigod (Epothos)	Demigod (Durlock)	Demigod (Helamis)	Demigod	8
God (Aenna)	God (Epothos)	God (Durlock)	God (Helamis)	God	10

wrath unleashed chapter 9

versus and team fighter modes

◆ *team fighter*
◆ *versus mode*

Note

Unlike in the Army Builder for Battle mode, you can have Elementals on your team in Team Fighter mode.

Once your team is constructed, highlight and select "OK?" on your section of the Build Team menu to proceed to the Fighter Select menu.

Fighter Select

VERSUS AND TEAM FIGHTER MODES

Note
The winner of a round of combat cannot choose a new creature, but must stick with the winning creature until it is killed in combat.

When the Team Fighter game is set up and your team is assembled, it's time to start the battle. Each player chooses one creature and then selects "Begin Battle?" at the bottom of the screen to start the match.

Select another fighter after each round you lose.

After the first round of combat is complete, return to the Fighter Select menu. The loser chooses another creature.

Note
Winning creatures do not regenerate any health between rounds of combat, but they do fully recover their magic energy.

A winner is you!

When one team is eliminated, the surviving team is declared the winner. Choose a "Rematch" with the same settings and teams, or choose "Quit" and return to the Build Team menu.

Note
Winning arena fights adds to your Battle Record total; when you reach 100 arena wins, you get the Defender medal and the Metal Age arena. When you win 20 Team Fighter mode matches–that is, when you win a Team Fighter game that is played to completion, with one team being destroyed–you're awarded the Tactician medal and the Elephant Pool combat arena is unlocked.

GAME SECRETS

wrath
unleashed
chapter 10

game secrets
◆ *cheat codes*
◆ *unlockable game
   features*

CHEAT CODES*

Title screen

*Versus mode Creature
Select menu*

Team Fighter mode Creature Select menu

The following four cheat codes dramatically change your *Wrath Unleashed* experience. You'll know when you entered the code correctly–the screen flashes and a distinctive sound is heard.

Note
Pay attention to the cheat code descriptions to find out where to enter the code. Some cheats need to be entered at the title screen, some at the Versus mode Creature Select menu, and some at the Team Fighter mode Creature Select menu.

*NOTICE: Use of cheat codes is not intended to allow for modification to the software. Use of the software remains subject to all terms and conditions of the software license & warranty. All unauthorised uses are strictly prohibited.

Large World Map Creatures

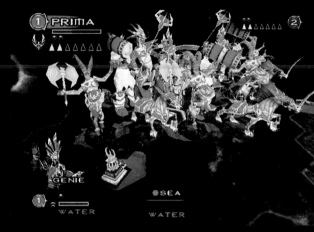

Large World Map creatures

This code makes creatures appear twice their usual size on the World Map. Enter the following at the *Wrath Unleashed* title screen:

XBOX CHEAT
Ⓛ, Ⓧ, Ⓛ, Ⓨ, Ⓛ►, Ⓑ, Ⓛ, Ⓑ

PS2 CHEAT
←, ■, ↑, ●, →, ▲, ↓, ▲

Hyper Extended Fighting

Hyper extended fighting (see the number of extra health orbs?

GAME SECRETS

When enabled, this cheat gives creatures more than twice their normal health, and *Wrath Unleashed* moves at more than twice its usual speed. This cheat only works in Versus and Team Fighter modes. If you start a war game (Battle or Campaign), the cheat is disabled. Enter the following cheat at the *Wrath Unleashed* title screen:

XBOX CHEAT

Ⓛ, Ⓛ, Ⓛ, Ⓛ, ◁Ⓛ, Ⓛ▷, Ⓛ, Ⓛ, Ⓛ, Ⓛ, Ⓛ, ◁Ⓛ, Ⓧ

PS2 CHEAT

↓, ↓, ↑, ↓, ←, →, ↓, ↑, ↑, ↑, →, ←, ■

Versus Mode Character Variations

Versus mode character variations

Tired of the same color schemes for your creatures in Versus mode? Enter the following code at the Versus mode Creature Select menu to enable three additional color combos for each realm's creatures; use "Cycle" (shown in the lower right corner) to change the color combinations.

XBOX CHEAT

Ⓛ, Ⓛ, Ⓛ, Ⓛ, ᴮᴸᴷ, ᵂᴴᵀ, ᴮᴸᴷ, ᵂᴴᵀ, Ⓡ, Ⓛ, ᴮᴸᴷ, Ⓡ, Ⓡ, ᵂᴴᵀ

XBOX CHEAT

Ⓛ, Ⓛ, Ⓛ, Ⓛ, ᴮᴸᴷ, ᵂᴴᵀ, ᴮᴸᴷ, ᵂᴴᵀ, Ⓡ, Ⓛ, ᴮᴸᴷ, Ⓡ, Ⓡ, ᵂᴴᵀ

PS2 CHEAT

L1, L1, ↓, ↓, R2, SELECT, R2, SELECT, R1, L1, R2, R1, R1, SELECT

Team Fighter Mode Character Variation

Team Fighter mode character variation

Like the character variation cheat in Versus mode, this cheat code lets you customize the color combinations of your realm's creatures in Team Fighter mode. Enter the following code at the Team Fighter mode Creature Select menu:

XBOX CHEAT

Ⓛ, Ⓛ, Ⓛ, Ⓛ, ᴮᴸᴷ, ᵂᴴᵀ, ᴮᴸᴷ, ᵂᴴᵀ, Ⓡ, Ⓛ, ᴮᴸᴷ, Ⓡ, Ⓡ, ᵂᴴᵀ

PS2 CHEAT

L1, L1, ↓, ↓, R2, SELECT, R2, SELECT, R1, L1, R2, R1, R1, R1, SELECT

PRIMA'S OFFICIAL STRATEGY GUIDE

UNLOCKABLE GAME FEATURES

Wrath Unleashed has plenty of hidden game features. Follow these instructions to fully unlock *Wrath Unleashed*.

Gods

*wrath
unleashed
chapter 10*

game secrets
- cheat codes
- unlockable game features

Each God is unlocked when that realm's Campaign missions are completed.

Each realm has a God Overlord that is even more powerful than the realm's Demigod Overlord. To unlock each realm's God, complete all four Campaign mode missions for that realm. Once unlocked, the God can be added to your custom army in Battle mode and chosen as a creature in Versus and Team Fighter modes.

Bonus Gallery

A fully unlocked Bonus Gallery

As you complete Campaign missions, you unlock images of *Wrath Unleashed* concept art in the Bonus Gallery. The following Campaign mode missions unlock the following images:

Light Order, Mission 1

Light Order, Mission 3

Light Chaos, Mission 1

Light Chaos, Mission 3

Dark Order, Mission 1

Dark Order, Mission 2

Dark Chaos, Mission 1

Dark Chaos, Mission 3

World Maps

Battle mode has four unlockable World Maps, which are unlocked under the following conditions:

Red 5 (2-Player): *Complete Light Order Campaign mission 2.*

Frenzy (2-Player): *Complete Light Chaos Campaign mission 2.*

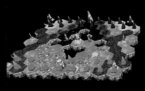

Grandmaster (2-Player): *Complete Dark Chaos Campaign mission 2.*

153

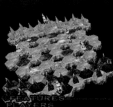

BATTLE   SELECT MAP

```
COLLISION
SPELLBOUND
NEUTRAL ZONE
SIPHON
PORTAL SHIFT
THE RACE
FRENZY
RED 5
GRANDMASTER
CHECKERED
```

```
FEATURES
PLAYERS           2
DIFFICULTY        INTERMEDIATE
TEMPLE TOTAL      6 POINTS
NEED TO WIN       6 POINTS
```

```
START GAME        BRIEFING
      Ⓐ SELECT Ⓑ BACK
```

Medals

LIGHT ORDER CAMPAIGN : AWARDED FOR COMPLETING ALL LIGHT ORDER MISSIONS.

Ⓑ EXIT

From left to right, top row: Light Order Campaign, Light Chaos Campaign, Realm Master, Dark Order Campaign, Dark Chaos Campaign. From left to right, bottom row: Strategist, Defender, Tactician.

Unlocking the medals doesn't change the gameplay experience, but the conditions for unlocking the medals are the same as those for unlocking hidden arenas, World Maps, and other locked features.

game secrets
- cheat codes
- unlockable game features

Checkered (2-Player): *Win more than 20 war games (Battle or Campaign missions).*

Battle Arenas

Two battle arenas can be unlocked and chosen for arena combat in Versus and Team Fighter modes:

Elephant Pool: *Win 20 Team Fighter mode matches.*

Metal Age: *Win 100 arena fights.*

CONDITIONS FOR EARNING MEDALS

Medal	Conditions for Unlocking
Light Order Campaign	Complete all Light Order Campaign missions.
Light Chaos Campaign	Complete all Light Chaos Campaign missions.
Dark Order Campaign	Complete all Dark Order Campaign missions.
Dark Chaos Campaign	Complete all Dark Chaos Campaign missions.
Realm Master	Complete all 16 Campaign missions.
Strategist	Win 20 Battle mode games.
Tactician	Win 20 Team Fighter matches.
Defender	Win 100 Battle Arena matches.

NOW AVAILABLE FROM PRIMA GAMES

SECRET WEAPONS OVER NORMANDY

PRIMA'S OFFICIAL STRATEGY GUIDE

- ★ Comprehensive tactics and historical information for all planes

- ★ Detailed flight training and combat strategies

- ★ Exhaustive walkthrough for all missions

- ★ Interview with Totally Games

- ★ Details every maneuver and combat tactic you'll need to determine the ultimate outcome of the Second World War

www.lucasarts.com
www.overnormandy.com

Levi Buchanan

primagames.com®